Copyright © 2012 by Adam Lawrence Smith and Jeff David Allen. All rights reserved.

Published by Intentional Vision Publishing

Book cover design by Dan Longhurst
Book layout, design and composition by Adam Lawrence Smith

No part of this publication may be reproduced, stored in a retrieval system, or transmitted in any form or by any means, electronic, mechanical, photocopying, recording, scanning, or otherwise, for the purpose of monetary or commercial gain, except as permitted under Section 107 or 108 of the 1976 United State Copyright Act, without either the prior written permission of the Publisher, or authorization through payment of appropriate per-copy fee to the Copyright Clearance Center, 222 Rosewood Drive, Danvers, MA 01923, (978) 750-8400, fax (978) 646-8600, or on the web at www.copyright.com. Publisher permission requests should be requested through contact information on kryptonitefactor.com.

Limit of Liability/Disclaimer of Warranty: While the publisher and the author have used their best efforts in preparing this book, they make no representation or warranties with respect to the accuracy or completeness of the contents of this book and specifically disclaim any implied warranties of merchantability or fitness for a particular purpose. No warranty may be created or extended by sales representatives or written sales materials. The advice and strategies contained herein may not be suitable for your situation. You should consult with a professional where appropriate. Neither the publisher nor the author shall be liable for any loss of profit or any other commercial damages, including but not limited to special, incidental, consequential, or other damages.

Library of Congress Cataloging-in-Publishing Data Adam Lawrence Smith and Jeff David Allen.
The Kryptonite Factor
p. cm.
ISBN 0615725198
1. Category Self Help
Printed in the United States of America

Table of Contents

Acknowledgements 6
   From Adam 6
   From Jeff 7
   From Both Authors 8

Preface 9
   About This Book 9
   How To Start Your Journey 9
   Author's Note: 11

Chapter 1 13
   Every Superhero Has A Weakness 13
   What Do You Fear Most? 15
   Fear and Pain 18
   Making It Crystal Clear 22
   Intentional Vision Exercises 22

Chapter 2 23
   Discovering Your Personal Identity 23
   Different Thinking Styles 27
   Three Levels of Thinking 28
   The Unconscious or Innate Mind 29
   The Subconscious or Imprinted Mind 32
   The Conscious or Intending Mind 33
   Recognizing Your Talents 34
   To Thine Own Self Be True 37
   Magnitude of Thinking Style 38
   Brain Quadrants 38
   Thinking Styles at a Glance 39
   Red – Urgent 41
   Orange – Activator 43
   Yellow – Optimist 45
   Blue – Awareness 47
   Teal – Logic 50
   Green – Realist 52
   Combinations and Opposites 54
   Making It Crystal Clear 57

  Intentional Vision Exercises 57

Chapter 3 58
  Trusting Life By Trusting God And The Universe 58
  Rude Awakening 65
  The Eagle Who Thought He Was A Chicken 70
  What Does Trusting Life Mean 73
  Blindsided By God's Plan 74
  My Experience With The Conversation With God 81
  Making It Crystal Clear 85
  Intentional Vision Exercises 85

Chapter 4 87
  Trust Your Powers And Discover Your Kryptonite 87
  The Guy In The Glass 87
  The Second Law – Trust Your Powers In The Universe . 89
  The Coach's Kryptonite 95
  Finding Kryptonite With Thai Food 98
  Owning Your Major Weakness 102
  Freedom and Forgiveness 105
  Mistakes Are My Friends 106
  Faith and Weakness 108
  Feed The Dragon – Embrace Your Major Weakness 111
  Personal Wins for the Week 113
  Making It Crystal Clear 118
  Intentional Vision Exercises 119

Chapter 5 121
  Trust That Your Neighbor Is Also A Superhero 121
  How Do You Play The Superhero or Victim Game? 130
  Co-Creative Conversations 141
  Co-Creative Vs. Parent-Child-Victim Relationships 144
  Ask Your Neighbor 149
  Making It Crystal Clear 152
  Intentional Vision Exercises 152

Chapter 6 154
  Your Kryptonite Is Embedded In Your Rules of Life 154
  Clarity of Freedom 157
  The Role of the Subconscious or Imprinted Mind 160
  Whose Rules And Stories Are These Anyway? 162
  Rewriting The Stories 168

Making It Crystal Clear 179
Intentional Vision Exercises 179

Chapter 7 180
Seeing With Superhero Vision................................. 180
What-You-See-Is-What-You-Get 180
Optical Illusions or Illusions of the Mind 180
Be a Superhero… Be a Leader................................. 183
Choosing To See It The Hard Way 194
Sex Isn't the Issue 197
I Can't Win Without You Behind Me 203
Goal Systems See And Emotionalize Success 207
Making It Crystal Clear 209
Intentional Vision Exercises 210

Chapter 8 211
Embracing Your Kryptonite – Owning Your Life 211
Don't Stop Seeing Angels and Superheroes................ 211
Finding the Lost Ring 220
Superman Owned His Wheelchair 222
Tale of Two Eagles 225
Embrace Your Kryptonite, You Become The Master 231
Final Affirmation 232
Making It Crystal Clear 234
Intentional Vision Exercises 234

Epilogue 235

Acknowledgements

From Adam

Whenever I wrote anything while going through school I always dreaded getting back my papers full of red marks and corrections. Once you read the book and understand my Kryptonite, you'll understand why I experience writing that way. However, once I entered my profession in marketing and instructional design, I quickly realized that writing is a team sport. I consider myself blessed with such a great team of people who have helped me write and refine this book. Without these people, this book doesn't happen.

First, I want to thank my wonderful family for their patience while I went through this process. They may have thought I was crazy, but as they keep seeing the principles I was learning show up in their lives, I continue to look wiser in their eyes. I also thank my family for repeating back principles whenever I needed a reminder of my truth. Children have a way of teaching their parents, if we will only listen to and watch for the lessons they teach us.

A special thanks goes to my beautiful wife who has allowed me to share some personal learning experiences we had together to hopefully help other people better understand a different way to look at life as well as all the people who have different personalities but similar intentions. My wife was also my first editor in this book writing process.

I want to thank my mother for instilling a curiosity and love for knowledge and my father for his words of encouragement that I can accomplish anything with enough work and persistence. My parent's lessons were my first and most enduring life motivational program.

I'd like to thank Jeff for the experience he led me through that make up the pages of this book and another yet to come. He is not just a teacher, but also a dear friend. Hopefully some of the gratitude

I feel for Jeff and the camaraderie we shared come through in the words I've written.

Finally, I'd like to thank that higher source of power, which I prefer to call God. I thank God for the abundance in my life and for the growth, co-creation and miracles I get to experience daily in life.

From Jeff

When man is looking for meaning they become a seeker of truth within the mysteries of life. Each seeker has their unique gifts and talents to accomplish their individual quest and yet in the end, the journey is mostly for the peace of mind to know God.

I am a seeker; I am a passionate seeker for the thought behind the thought or the meaning of the present day physical manifestations most call reality.

And with a thankful heart I am in gratitude for the seekers of past, present and future. Their insights, nuances and clues to my journey in life that has made my life a rich experience. Adam is one of those seekers. You see, when the student is ready the teacher shows up and I am so thankful Adam, with his unique gifts and talents, came into my life when he did. He continues to teach me and be an important part of my life.

My life is filled with many great people and the richness of this cannot be described by simple words. First and foremost, I am thankful for God. I am thankful for my parents, siblings, and the small town I grew up in that gave me many rich childhood experiences that have become a large part of who I am.

I am grateful for my wife and 10 children for their tolerance and love as I have pursued my passions.

To be in gratitude is an acknowledgement that you are loved. It is with this gratitude that I am reverenced by the offering of love given by so many in my life. I offer you an abundance of love and gratitude on your quest as you seek your truth and that your efforts will be rewarded the purest praises of gratitude that life has to offer.

Be a lover of life and live in your pursuit of happiness with an abundance of gratitude.

From Both Authors

We both want to thank our students. In Jeff's case that would be thousands over the years he's been a life strategies coach. One thing Jeff has always said is that when the teacher is ready, the student appears and when the student is ready, the teacher appears. The teacher learns as much from the student as the student learns from the teacher. So thanks to everyone who has gone through this life strategies course for allowing the teachers to learn and helping this learning journey progress.

The editing contributors to this book include Linda Swain who helped reshape the content by suggesting a major rearrangement. Barbara Jensen, who was also a student, made a big difference in urging us to complete the work and influenced the tone when she provided her editing insights. And then there is Brent Bluth, who took us to the finish line and refined the way we described the process.

A big thanks also goes to Dan Longhurst for creating the striking cover artwork and design. There were many iterations of the design and in the end we're very happy with how it turned out.

Finally, we thank you, the reader, for making our experience a part of yours. May your experience bring you more of what you desire and joy in whatever you choose to do.

Preface

About This Book

This book follows the experiences of one author who goes through a life coaching process with the other author. The coaching process is referred to in the book as the Intentional Vision process. This book represents the first half of the Intentional Vision process and the core for making any lasting change in life – gaining trust for life, yourself and in others. Each person has a different personality and therefore different weaknesses and strengths.

This book explores how you can define your major weakness or fear to help you use it as a learning tool to unleash your innate strengths. By embracing your major weakness or your kryptonite, you will learn to trust life, self and others at a deeper level and be able to move on to learn how to love and co-create your dreams and purpose in life.

How To Start Your Journey – Awareness > Agreement > Action

You can gain a great amount of knowledge and awareness from reading this book as you can with many other self-help books. Over time your increased awareness may help you to change your behavior, habits and life. Each time you read you learn something new; you have new neural networks that are laid down. As long as they aren't in serious conflict with other beliefs you have, these new neural networks can coexist. But will these new neural networks change your life? Not necessarily – not unless you decide to weed out your limiting beliefs and replace them with self-empowering ones. In order to rewrite these limiting beliefs you have to follow a different process.

The way to create new, empowering beliefs is to follow this process – Awareness -> Agreement -> Action. When you gain a new awareness, make an agreement as to what purpose you're going to use your new awareness for and then take immediate action. This process of Awareness, Agreement, and Action will rewrite old negative patterns in your mind and lay down new, stronger patterns of belief.

The Intentional Vision process for this book is fairly simple. You need to read to gain awareness. Then make an agreement that you will reread every day for a week a short section (usually one to three pages) about a Law of Intentional Vision you are working on. Then take action by doing a few exercises at the end of each chapter. It really is a very simple way to reprogram your mind to be creative, curious and to experience more abundance and love without the fear and scarcity.

Here is the recommended way to follow the Intentional Vision process through this book:

1) Read through the book once – Highlight ideas that jump out at you and do at least one of the exercises at the end of each of the chapters.

2) Reread to reprogram – Reread the gray sections of each chapter and whatever notes or highlighted concepts that struck you the most during the your first reading. Read one reading assignment at least five days each week and continue to make notes about the 'ahas!' that occur. Do this until you've completed the book a second time. Starting with your personality profile, this should take you six to seven weeks.

3) Keep a success (wins) or gratitude journal – Identify and record all the wins you have each week as you go through this reading experience. A win represents your increased awareness and is anything you consciously or intentionally desire that is manifested in your reality, either by direct action or by sheer belief. Getting your mind in the habit of finding wins in life is key to seeing all the miracles that naturally occur in your everyday experience.

4) *Make this your experience* – Write all the thoughts that come to you in the margins or in a success journal as you read. You will soon start to read a personal meaning into every page, paragraph and sentence. In this way, the book becomes your experience and the ideas that spring up are yours. New neural-connections will be written each time you choose to read your assignments and new

information will begin to come from everywhere in your life to synch up with what you're reading.

5) ***Include your friends or neighbors and increase your success*** – If you choose, find a friend who will share the experience with you and read it at the same time. Get together, share your wins, discuss your positive experiences, and help coach each other through the experience. Your neighbor or friend is the best mirror you have so you can look at your thoughts through someone else's eyes.

Warning: If you choose to go through the weekly assignments, whatever you do, DO NOT GIVE UP AFTER 21-30 DAYS! Whoever said that it takes 21 days to create a habit was only partly right. We've seen a consistent pattern in people who are working to create wins in their life, who more often than not have challenges to their newly forming habits around 21-30 days. It's as if the old patterns don't want to die and they put up a fight. You may have already experienced this with other positive habits you've tried to form. We'll help you overcome this with a greater awareness and action. Just keep moving forward, no matter what, until you reach the end and the pay off will be huge in how you look at life and naturally attract positive experiences.

Author's Note:

You may not believe everything in this book and that's okay. Again, I want to make it clear that this is not a religious book (although various beliefs are presented as a way to trust life at a greater level), but it does touch on spiritual things. Spiritual in this sense means the things of the heart or your core emotions and innate life powers. As you discover more about yourself through the Intentional Vision program, you'll understand why some information is designed and presented for different personality types. Believe what you want, use what you want, but in the end, this was my experience and it is how

I chose to see and document my journey through the Intentional Vision process.

I believe there is no accident you have this book right now and I strongly believe the power to change your life is in your hands. I'm certain that by going through the Intentional Vision process, you will experience many of the same emotions and successes I did, unique and powerful to your personality.

If you choose to follow the Intentional Vision process, to create new strategies in your life, you will be one of many who experience a whole different kind of growth in your life, in your beliefs, and in your ability to manifest abundance in all facets of life. I hope you will enjoy this journey. It is my intention and desire that you find a way to enjoy more Intentional Vision in your life. If you desire to experience even greater depth in awareness and ways to make stronger agreements with yourself and putting them into action, please refer to any of the following web sites: www.kryptonitefactor.com, www.intentionalvision.com and www.winningpersonalities.com

As you start here and choose this journey to live an amazing life, I hope to meet you someday, so I can share the road with you and our stories with each other. Until then, 'Up, Up and Away!' and Make It a Great Day!

Chapter 1

Every Superhero Has A Weakness

"You cannot run away from a weakness; you must sometimes fight it out or perish. And if that be so, why not now, and where you stand?"
– Robert Louis Stevenson

You probably never thought you had something in common with Superman. He had a major weakness – kryptonite. It was a green crystal that came from his home planet of Krypton. For some reason, this green crystal would sap all of Superman's energy and make him weaker than a human; so weak, it would nearly destroy him. I always thought it was strange that a little green crystal from Superman's home planet could actually make him weaker and not stronger. Why is that? From all accounts, this was Superman's only weakness, and yet, every time he nearly meets his doom, kryptonite somehow is a part of the story.

Almost every time I mention to someone that they have a major weakness, they respond, "Which one... I have so many of them." What if all of your weaknesses and your bad habits stemmed from one fear that is implanted in your mind? Would that change the way you think about yourself and the way you went about figuring out how to make major self-improvements?

I've always looked at myself as someone with both strengths and weaknesses. I assumed everyone felt the same way. What I didn't realize until I went through the Intentional Vision Life Coaching process with Jeff Allen is that everyone has a major weakness, a chink in the armor, an Achilles heel. I was taken back when Jeff said, "*The source of every negative program or habit you have, or automatic negative program, is attached to your major weakness... every single one!*"

Although Superman's major weakness is kryptonite, not everyone has the same major weakness. Each person experiences this fear differently based on their personality and the way their minds are wired. In fact, the major weakness might be much the same for you and someone else with a similar personality, but the way you give it a name and describe it might be different. The point of this book is to help you discover three things:

1) Your major weakness or fear and how by embracing this weakness or fear you can learn faster, experience greater spiritual growth and develop more passion and love in your life

2) How developing trust with life, self and others is the key to unlocking your strengths that are hidden by your major weakness

3) To embrace who you are, both weaknesses and strengths, and become the master of your life, so you can teach others how to learn from their major weakness

First let's take a look at some of the fears we have and then we'll dive deeper to find the underpinning fears that show up as your major weakness.

What Do You Fear Most?

Unlike other superheroes, Superman is his true self when he's being a superhero. Other superheroes are always acting as their alter egos when they are in the superhero mode. Superman disguises himself as Clark Kent, a human without much courage. He's showing many other weaknesses, so he can cover his strength. How many of us do the same in life?

In a similar way, we hide our potential and divine nature from others and ourselves. In order not to offend others, we have taken a secular view and removed the divine from our conversations. A passage from Marianne Williamson's book, *Return to Love,* is often misquoted about what we fear most. Miss Williamson's quote was used by Nelson Mandela in his inaugural speech. Her message was also used in the movie, *Coach Carter,* starring Samuel L. Jackson, who asked the question to a student, "What do you fear most?" But the real irony is why people misquote Marianne Williamson. It is due to the very fear that is mentioned in the quote – the fear of our divine nature. Most people who quote Marianne Williamson leave out the divine message of being a child of the Creator, which is core to who we are and from where we came.

Here is Marianne Williamson's quote as she wrote it:

"Our deepest fear is not that we are inadequate. Our deepest fear is that we are powerful beyond measure. It is our light, not our darkness, that most frightens us. We ask ourselves, who am I to be brilliant, gorgeous, talented and fabulous?

Actually, who are you not to be?

You are a child of God. Your playing small doesn't serve the world. There's nothing enlightened about shrinking so that other people won't feel insecure around you.

We were born to make and manifest the glory of God that is within us. It's not just in some of us; it's in everyone. And as we let our own light shine, we unconsciously give other people permission to do the same. As we are liberated from our own fear, our presence automatically liberates others."
– Marianne Williamson, *Return to Love*

Superman is more often afraid of his strengths and true self being exposed than he is about anything else. In fact, all superheroes are afraid of the same thing – having their powers and true identity exposed. My question is, like Superman, why are we afraid to talk about our divine nature and amazing powers? Are you willing to openly talk about it? The very essence of this quote tells us why. We are afraid of the light that resides within us, so we let fear of what others might think edit the deeper meaning of the quote, just as we often let fear edit the deeper meaning of our lives and our love from everyone around us, including ourselves. We are all endowed with this same light, God's love.

It doesn't matter what divine source or belief system you believe in. You may even be an atheist and only believe in the power you have within – which scientifically we are finding is infinite. But give people the opportunity to express their faith and intention without judgment, and this world will see accelerated growth in every facet of the human experience.

Can you experience the peace of mind and spirit from the Zen masters? Can you see the power from Muhammad of obeying and following your beliefs at all costs? Can you see the beauty of giving up your fears and past mistakes to Christ? Can you feel the sanctity of life from the Hindus? Can you understand the everlasting hope of the Jews? Can you begin to sense the beauty in the earth and sky from those who worship them? Wouldn't you agree that there is beauty, purpose and love at the roots of all these enlightened trees of faith? They all give strength to the intention of humanity. Where is the person who will seek what's good between him or her and not what's different?

A man who inspired me to follow my dream and helped me seize the opportunity, told me that you either "worship or perish." And this principle of "worship or perish" in reality is what all religious writings are about. In a broader sense of his words "worship or perish," I took it that we have to experience trust, love and intention in this life in order to grow. If you aren't growing, you're perishing. So if you are not growing spiritually, you will be decreasing in this life experience.

Spiritual growth is about overcoming fear and creating more love and freedom. For some, more love might be base-jumping off cliffs or hiking in the mountains, gathering with family or attending a church service. Everyone needs a definable process for experiencing love and connecting to the divine and each person experiences it in a different way. Once you understand more clearly how your process of spirituality works, you will allow others to do the same. Each person has the right to worship God, but do you allow others to worship God too?

Mahatma Gandhi said this upon his return to India from England in 1931, "I am not conscious of a single experience throughout my three months stay in England and Europe that made me feel that after all East is East and West is West. On the contrary, I have been convinced more than ever that human nature is much the same, no matter under what clime it flourishes, and that if you approached people with trust and affection you would have ten-fold trust and thousand-fold affection returned to you." Gandhi made this statement after being thronged in admiration by the same people who were out of work because of his teachings to be self reliant in India. And yet, the majority of the common British citizens loved Gandhi for the truths he taught.

We have lost touch or forgotten our innate powers as divine creatures. Instead, we choose to be driven by fear instead of love. What is fear? What you fear is really what you don't know or understand or something that you've forgotten or lost trust in. How does fear show up? It shows up as things we think are evil or as things that bring up pain. In the end, it is our brains that conceive the fear as a way to protect us. Understanding fear and pain is part of understanding and embracing our kryptonite.

Fear and Pain

So what is pain? If we talk about physical pain, it is the body's way of preventing harm or experiencing loss or death. In other words, it is a form of fear. If a person's nervous system is damaged to the point where he can't feel his hand, he won't sense the fear of harm if something hot is held to his skin. The only reason he would withdraw his hand from the danger is if he sees it and the visual stimulus causes him the fear of loss. Pain can also be suffered at a mental or spiritual level and manifest itself in the body. Let me give you an example:

My uncle Randall has been a world-class athlete and is an extremely healthy individual. He used to compete at very high levels in snow skiing and water skiing. Then he took up motocross and flat track racing. He's also been involved in bicycling for more than a decade. More recently he decided to learn to surf and practice karate. He's in his early sixties and he's still approaching new dreams and goals with energy and intention. He's been a great example to me throughout my life.

My uncle had his share of accidents and I know he's broken several bones in many places in his body. However, it wasn't until he was in his later 40's that he began to experience back pain for some unknown reason. It was in his lower back and it was excruciating to the point that it started to prevent him from doing the activities he loved to do.

My uncle sought out chiropractors and doctors to help him solve his back problem. He went through the pain of several aggressive therapies. Finally, after years of intense pain, my uncle conceded to having back surgery. The surgery eased the pain, but there was still plenty to deal with. A friend referred a book to him, *The Mindbody Prescription* by John E. Sarno, M.D.

In his book, Dr. Sarno says that he's treated hundreds of patients for back pain and herniated discs. In the majority of the cases (88%), it only took an awareness of their emotions and beliefs to rectify the problem and the pain.

My uncle read the book once and didn't give it much credit; then he went back through the book and realized that the personalities described who had the back problems sounded a lot like him. He read the book again and the simple awareness that his subconscious mind was creating the pain made the pain miraculously disappear.

Jeff Allen also introduced me to a client of his who had gone through the death of someone the client considered to be her soul mate, then she suffered through a ruined rebound relationship, and found herself in a separate legal battle that threatened to destroy her professional legal career and disbar her from practicing law. She felt like she was near suicide. For no apparent reason, with no physical activity, she sustained a crushed disc in her back. Her emotions were so heavy that she physically manifested the pressure in her back. She came to Jeff, went through the Intentional Vision process and began to own her life. The pain went away, the threatening relationship left, and she was able to turn around how she viewed the legal action and was able to stand up for herself, where otherwise she wouldn't have.

Another researcher who is finding many astonishing details about the human body is a microbiologist named Dr. Bruce Lipton, who has studied the make up and behavior of the human cell. His findings lead us to believe that each cell changes based on the environment. And what changes the chemical environment the most is the brain and its beliefs.

When I understood that every cell responds and adapts to its environment – not necessarily its DNA, the hairs on the back of my neck stood up and my entire body resonated with the idea – which I'm sure were my cells reacting to my new beliefs. This means that our entire makeup, down to the basic building blocks of our bodies, are affected by our beliefs, our intentions. And that means *we are bodies of faith and intention, we are truly living a spiritual experience.* It's no wonder people can be healed by faith, no matter what belief system they have.

As soon as this idea was lodged in my mind, it made me think of the miracles of Christ. In nearly every case, he either asked whether the person had the faith to be healed or he sensed it, before healing them. I wonder if the power to be healed was within them, and in us, all along, and Christ along with other enlightened beings, are able to trigger that belief to be miraculously healed. At least it appears that the experienced miracles were a co-healing event.

Dr. Lipton further describes that if you understand how our bodies and any living organism operate, even down to single cell organisms, each organism either operates in a growth mode or a protective mode. With multi-cellular organisms, certain portions may be in growth mode while other areas may be in a protective mode. However, when the fear of death strikes hard, when the need to survive kicks in, the entire organism will take on a protective mode.

Here's what we can further conclude, that fear puts the mind, body and spirit in a protective mode. Take for instance how the mind and body work with the body's nutritional needs. The body's ability to store fat for future use is an example of how the body might live in fear. You could even say that fat is fear for the future. It's the body's mechanism for storing reserves for future lean times, which may never come. And how do our thoughts and fears affect the food we digest? Why is it that we are so afraid of food these days? We indulge ourselves in artificial or chemical stimulants, including food, and then we beat up on ourselves for everything we eat and drink. How many people fear food in one way or another?

Jeff Allen had another client, who I'll call Sheryl, come in during one of my sessions. Jeff always created an openness with his clients to help them share their life experiences with others, especially with other clients. However, he would withhold names and details about people to preserve their anonymity until you had the opportunity to meet the client and they were able to share their experiences with you.

Jeff told me beforehand how Sheryl used to be a much larger person. It wasn't until she had overcome some of her self-defeating patterns and overwritten her fears that she began to lose a tremendous amount of weight. Part of it was just looking at the food in a different way. She wasn't worried about or constantly thinking about the food as much.

As Sheryl visited with us, Jeff brought up her Caribbean cruise, "Oh, I forgot to ask, how was your cruise?"

Sheryl began talking about some of her friends who went with her. She also talked about the tables and tables of the finest food you could imagine. Sheryl said, "When my friends saw that I was really excited to go to one of the banquets, you know what they said? 'That food is terrible – it'll just make you fat.'"

Sheryl's response to her friends was, "Why would you curse the food even before you eat it? It's great food and I'm going to enjoy what I want to eat." She then said that she ate decent sized portions and really enjoyed every bite and she surprisingly lost a few pounds on the trip. Meanwhile, her same friends who made the negative remarks ended up gaining between five and ten pounds each on the trip. Sheryl summarized the point when she said, "We should bless the food we eat and not curse it." In other words, if we fear our food, our body goes into a protective state and will not utilize the food in the same abundant way another person might use it.

Fear and all its related sources kills more people in this world than anything else. It kills the body by reducing its functionality by causing it to overreact or shut down certain biological processes. Fear is why the body stores fat – to be ready when the body needs the extra energy during lean times. It brings on or fuels diseases and syndromes of every scientific name. Fear causes significant development problems for children both inside and outside the womb. Fear kills people through conflict and wars, because people fear and destroy what they don't know. Fear kills the spirit of men and women and leaves them feeling victims of a harsh cruel world. Fear kills, and if you can find and root out your fears, overwrite them, you will live a longer, healthier and happier life.

Yet fear is locked in a symbiotic relationship with love, and without it, we can't understand love, just as without darkness, we can't fully appreciate the light.

Making It Crystal Clear

Here are the finer points about everyone's kryptonite:

Everyone has a major weakness and it correlates with their personality and the way their brains are programmed

1) Your major weakness is really a strength if you embrace it and learn from it.
2) We often fear finding ourselves and our potential or divine nature.
3) Our brains are designed to protect us and pain is a form of fear written in our minds to protect us.
4) Fear is the root of all that destroys us.

Intentional Vision Exercises

Perform the following exercises every day for a week:

1) First Step To Understanding Your Kryptonite – Clear the clutter – Write down all the ways you have criticized yourself or others. Don't take too much time; just write down what comes to mind.
2) Then throw the list away or destroy it and say the words aloud, "I'm through with these negative emotions!" You will do this exercise for a week. If you do this, you will find that the list will grow smaller and eventually you'll come down to a few items to resolve, which is much easier to deal with.

Chapter 2

Discovering Your Personal Identity and Thinking Style

*This above all: to thine own self be true,
And it must follow, as the night the day,
Thou canst not then be false to any man.*
– Shakespeare's *Hamlet*

Superman knows his strengths as do most superheroes. He also trusts himself as he's using his strengths. Your journey to knowing who you are starts now! If you want freedom from fear, then you have to trust. You are unique, a miracle in the universe. "Why am I unique?" you ask. You are an amazing creation within the universe with the ability and power to co-create with God and the Universe.

You were not a blank slate when you came to this existence. You came to this life already programmed with your own powers to begin experiencing life in your own way. Your powers come from your personality and characteristics that were built right in.

Your parents handed their thought patterns and beliefs on to you. However, you have a choice, as you do with everything about this life experience, to keep what they gave you or create new patterns of thought to fit your needs and purpose.

Yes, you have a purpose here. You are here to learn and grow in wisdom and spiritual feelings of being connected to God and the Universe that created, provides, supports and loves you. You are also here to co-create anything you want with God and the Universe and in doing so; you will discover how you can truly experience love. What love is to me is not the same to you and that's one of the reasons why we're both unique in how we co-create.

You may be someone who experiences life through a physical process and doing things. You may be someone who thinks deeply, pondering the ways of life. You may be someone who connects deeply with others, and in doing things for others you feel this connection. You may be someone who simply likes to observe and teach what you've learned. In all these ways or paths, you are a creator and in the moment of doing, thinking or being, you have the opportunity to experience love – even God's love.

Because you were created with such powerful potential and life is truly about a spiritual journey, the only reason we have fears and doubts is to help us learn to be who we really are. And without this learning tool – fear – you would not understand your abilities, others' abilities, or the opportunities the Universe provides. This moment is the perfect opportunity, a gift to you – co-created and predetermined by your choices to discover what makes you who you are and what makes you happy. Have fun with this journey because it will become anything you choose it to be. If it's more love, more money, more freedom you want, then choose it. Life is short, but God gives you time to do the things you choose to co-create in the universe. In fact, when you are co-creating with purpose, you will lose all track of time.

Take an opportunity to look in the mirror. Right now would be great. What do you see? Can you see your physical body that was designed specifically for your spiritual growth? Also look deep into your eyes; look until you feel your soul. Can you feel it? Can you feel the warmth? Can you feel the love for yourself? Can you see that you are connected to this divine Universe of creation for your purpose and the purpose of co-creating love in the Universe? If looking in the mirror is uncomfortable to you, then you simply have a thinking pattern or belief that is hiding your true self from you. You are seeing Clark Kent and not Superman or Diana and not Wonder Woman.

Right at this moment, your body is recreating itself. Cells are being created to replace ones that have served their purpose. The air you breath is providing the connection to the Universe that keeps you alive. Your heart is not only pushing blood out to every cell in your body, it is providing a rhythm, a harmonious connection or communication to every cell in your body. The energy your body carries also has a unique vibration, different than anyone else on the planet. It is your soul signature. Yes, you are as unique of a creation in the universe as any planet or star, which also have their own unique vibration from their creation.

So I ask you, what is it that you are to do with this opportunity, this journey you're on? What is your purpose? It will be hard to know, unless you know yourself, trust yourself, love and honor yourself, care for yourself and appreciate yourself. Take time each day to look in the mirror and behold the wonder of the Universe that you are. Look deep in your soul and see the person you have created, the person God created, and the person you and God are co-creating.

Choices happen in an instant, you can choose now to live and be you, the ultimate you, or you can choose to do nothing. You could choose to have your next year of life be like the last one or you can choose to take it to the next level of love and creation. Don't run from yourself – that is truly a tiring journey. It's time for you to know yourself. It's time to choose to be the real you. Carpe Diem Amore! Seize the day with love!

You can search throughout the entire universe for someone who is more deserving of your love and affection than you are yourself, and that person is not to be found anywhere. You yourself, as much as anybody in the entire universe deserve your love and affection.
— Buddha

You have a purpose in this life experience, whether you believe it's something you just have or because you feel God or a supreme being gave it to you. But how do you make it real and lasting? Knowing your purpose in life is an important key to making this life experience worthwhile, but before you can truly find your purpose in life, you have to find and understand yourself first. You have to find out who you are, what motivates you, and why you are the person you are at this point in time. If you want to be successful – however you choose to define success – you must know where you're going and you must understand yourself, your strengths and what it will take for you to enjoy your journey toward success.

People who don't have an intended outcome or personal goals don't trust themselves to succeed. They always question themselves and find it hard to make decisions. For instance, ask someone, "If you could have something more in life, what would it be?" There are many who would give you answers like, "more free time and more money," but it will be almost impossible for them to tell you, with enough confidence, who they are and how they own their life.

Knowing who you are is the foundation, the base, the beginning of self-development. People who know themselves on a deep level often find themselves accomplishing many victories with less effort, fear and pain. People who become great always use talents and strengths they possess in their personality. As you become clear about your identity, you will make changes in how you think and how you communicate, to create the success and the life you want – that you were born to experience.

If you were created in this life experience to fulfill a purpose you chose and your mind (the mind including both the brain and heart) is what guides you through this journey, then it is important to know at a greater depth who you really are. You came to this existence with certain innate programs already there. Just ask any mother if her children are different from each other when they were born or even in the womb. Next, you were socialized by larger people in your experience, primarily your parents, and the experiences you had while growing up. These patterns are imprinted upon your mind and can either limit your success and beliefs or accelerate them. The last part is how you perceive your ideal self to be and how you want to present yourself to the outside world. These three areas of your personality make up what we call your identity profile, which gives you a better picture of what motivates you at both the conscious and sub-conscious levels of your thinking.

Different Thinking Styles

Can I create the life I want and how do I do it? Is there more out there, or am I living the life I'm destined for? The individuals we view as successful and happy learned at some point in their life how to create their results. Yes, that's correct, "learned". That means you can learn to create the results you want too. Ultimately you're constantly searching for deeper meaning and understanding, wondering how you can achieve your success and experience a level of purpose that is fulfilling. This type of searching is part of our spiritual journey through this life experience.

Let's claim that the cycle of this life is designed to continually pass on knowledge and information through an eternal, even a spiritual, progression. Under this pretense, it is important to understand that a parent to child exchange becomes purposeful and significant – whether it be a positive or a negative experience.

Science has already identified that our responses to life are more closely related to belief systems that have been passed down from generation to generation than they are to actual genetics. For example, the eating habits and emotional attachment to food that parents pass on has more of an effect on a child's weight than do genetic traits.

At times we create the results we want, and at other times we create the results we don't want due to self-sabotage. Self-sabotage is a very common by-product of the translations we made and continue to make about the events that took place very early in our life. Self-sabotage is the result of negative patterns we keep stored in our minds to relate to similar events that come up. Through much study and research, we are now able to find ways to overcome these self-defeating programs we've built within our minds.

Each person is a combination of the character traits they came to earth with, those that were taught to them, and the characteristics that they develop as they grow and mature and decide what they value most in life. Because of all these different factors to what makes you the person you are, it's important to look in a mirror, so to speak, and see who you are.

Three Levels of Thinking

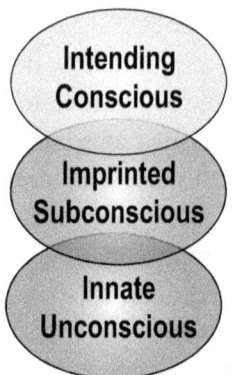

There are three separate levels of awareness: conscious, subconscious, and unconscious. To give you an example of how these different levels of awareness work, let's consider someone in a swimming pool. If they try to drown themselves by just thinking they can hold their breath until they pass out, their bodies won't let them. This is the unconscious or innate mind at work. Some might even call it your life force or spirit. An example of the subconscious mind or imprinted self working is the way you might look at how your parents brought you up and you say to yourself that you'll never do it like they did, and then you repeat many of the patterns your parents imprinted on you. These stored patterns that are imprinted on us have a strong influence on our everyday behavior. You could also think of this as your self-conscious, much like the depiction of a little angel or a little devil on your shoulder, whispering thoughts in your ear. Finally, there is the conscious mind or intending self. This is about your ideas and how you think through and solve challenges in various areas of your life.

As you can see, the three levels of consciousness are used in different situations. Each level of consciousness will have its own dominant method to solve problems and patterns of reasoning in life. You've probably noticed people who act a certain way when around friends and associates, but then take on a completely different persona when they are in their home or work environment. It is important to understand that we each have three different personal identities we use in different environments.

The Unconscious or Innate Mind

The strongest and most important identity is your unconscious or innate mind. The innate mind is the natural personality that came with you as you started this life. It is truly the foundation of who you are just like you came with programs in your brain to know how to suckle. It is also programmed with the fabric of the universe or the universal laws of divine creation. You are programmed or driven to follow these governing laws. Because you are a creation of the universe and operate under the same governing laws, the innate mind responds by needing to love and be loved. It also drives the need to have self-agency or the ability to choose and not be forced. This program in the innate mind is also the one that consistently needs to create, expand and become greater, like the Universe. If you don't fulfill these unconscious needs and desires, you will quickly become stuck in life and attract lessons to help reconnect you to the universal laws.

If the universal laws, which are written into your innate mind, are not satisfied, you will never be able to achieve long lasting happiness or reach your full potential. The innate mind is where your inner feelings and confidence come from. The innate is the natural you and it operates more like a computer that only responds to the programs in it and the input it receives.

The innate part of the brain is the core of who you are and is considered unconscious, because it is below conscious thinking and its dominant language is feelings. It is those innermost feelings and desires that are hard to put words to in order to describe. It communicates based on fear and love or a sense of safety or acceptance. Think of any newborn baby; it needs to have a feeling of acceptance and love to survive. Newborns also need to feel safe from harm or danger or the avoiding of fear. The innate mind has all the safety and survival programs in it and when you feel fear, this is the mind that engages and overrides the other minds. If any of the universal laws are not being satisfied and you're not feeling love, your innate mind thinks you're not surviving.

The innate mind is what senses your entire body down to the cellular level. It takes in all of the body as if it were an entire collective conscious. Within the innate mind are complex programs that control your body's most basic needs for survival-programs such as your breathing, heartbeat, muscle control, chemical balance and maintaining physical wellness. The innate mind also contains many of your survival and safety programs causing you to behave a certain way when you are in danger because of hunger, thirst and physical pain. It helps protect your life. When your 'fight or flight' response kicks in because of perceived danger, your unconscious is running the show, because the primary blood flow has gone to the muscles and away from the brain. When this happens it is virtually impossible to be consciously thinking, you are reacting innately, protecting life. Because all of these programs are necessary for survival from the moment you are born, the unconscious is very rigid, obsessive and ritualistic.

The innate mind can be processing information and running without you consciously thinking about what it's doing. It is a vast majority of your brainpower and runs hundreds of times faster than the conscious thinking brain. This personality is innate; it's the one nature gave you. The innate mind repeats not only survival programs that keep the body parts and chemistry functioning over and over, but also repeats the behavior programs again and again as well. These repeating programs are defined and reinforced during the earliest years of your life, based on the problem solving methods enforced by significant people in your life. The same time you are persuaded to conform to rules in life, you are also determining the best way for you to personally find safety based on your unconscious programs. These programs are so ingrained; the innate mind automatically processes the information and responds so quickly that many times you react before thinking.

A good example of the innate mind overtaking to provide safety is if you touch something hot; you will jump away before thinking.

Because the unconscious controls our nature, the innate mind can be like an emotional 800-pound gorilla. When out of control, it can be very destructive, but when used effectively it can be a source of enormous emotional, psychological and spiritual strength. Identifying your innate identity is a significant step in controlling the emotional 800-pound gorilla. By knowing who you are at the core, you will understand what you need to do to keep the innate mind satisfied and feeling safe. When the innate mind is satisfied, you begin to feel the magic life has to offer. It allows the "juice' or "mojo" of life to come out and flow. It will help you get in the "zone." The innate mind will allow you to feel joy and satisfaction when the innate is safe and being nurtured by its surroundings. If it is not feeling safe and protected, it will constantly remind you through your feelings that you are fearful and lack trust in your environment. You will find that things come easy, and you are able to enjoy success often when feeling safe and using your innate mind properly.

Furthermore, as your self-awareness increases, you'll begin to see some of the ingrained programs that are hindering your happiness and contradict who you would like to be. Although the innate is the hardest to communicate to, you can learn to rewrite the imprinted programs that inhibit your ability to use amazing powers of the innate mind.

The positive aspects of the innate mind are most commonly expressed in the home environment, unless it's a hostile environment, when it is not seeking approval or a need to defend itself. You feel more like yourself when you can tap into the limitless powers of your innate mind. When your innate mind feels accepted and safe in your environment, you will have courage, confidence, trust, and love and you will be able to use more of the powers and abilities of the innate mind.

The Subconscious or Imprinted Mind

The imprinted identity or mind is sub-conscious or just below your conscious thought. The subconscious or imprinted thinking style is the part of the conscious that is learned, and is what nurturing gave you. The information stored in the imprinted was mostly programmed before the age of 6, but can be programmed or reprogrammed later in life. The later you choose to reprogram the imprinted mind, the more effort will be required. This thinking style is primarily programmed because it wanted acceptance or to feel safe in relationships and the environment. For example, this is the part of the brain that would remember the emotional pain associated with being burned, or being spanked, or being disciplined.

This imprinted area in your mind stores many of the programs that trigger high emotions of fear and doubt, which hold you back in your life. The imprinted operates like a computer that has been programmed from the past. It responds to situations using patterns or programs that have been learned through your early life experiences. These programs run repeatedly, trying to avoid pain or gain pleasure or love. These emotional programs are memories of past experiences that are both good and bad, but are in constant lookout to protect you from repeating experiences of pain from the past. The most critical factor with the imprinted mind is that many of its programs were created in times of stress and pain. It is constantly holding a memory of the event trying to compare past to present, wanting to avoid the past pain. The complexity of this is that it cannot distinguish between past younger childhood fears and the conscious adult coping skills.

For example, you might have had one of your family members put you to bed, turn the light off, and shut the door. Now as an adult you might still have memories of the fear associated with the dark and feeling lonely. As an adult we should be able to consciously say, "I shouldn't feel afraid of the dark," because we know that the environment is safe, but when we hear a strange noise or creak in the house, the old programs from our childhood are running too, making it hard to overcome the feelings of fear we had as a child. As you can see, you can have several programs running at the same time that are commonly from the imprinted mind that needs to create safety.

The imprinted mind seems to have a voice and it is usually the voice of your parents or the bigger people who affected your early childhood development. It can even cause significant conflict in your mind with an argument (the angel and devil on the shoulder idea) between your innate and your imprinted minds. These imprinted patterns are learned and used because it is an internal control mechanism looking for methods to provide an emotionally safe environment and ways to be accepted in relationships. It also holds your standards, rules and belief systems of how you are nurturing or treating others correctly.

Because the imprinted is tightly connected to the innate, the imprinted also has many programs that are actively running without focused thinking. Instead of being innate, these programs are ones you learned through repetition. The imprinted is where all your habits are stored. Let's take driving a car as an example. Rarely do you actively think about pushing the gas pedal, turning the steering wheel, or the route you take to get home from work. Your imprinted kicks in and performs all those functions while your conscious mind is busy with other things.

The Conscious or Intending Mind

The conscious part of your brain is the thinking style you develop most in your teenage and young adult years. It is your focused thinking. It is the style that we present the most to others when we are feeling safe and trust ourselves and the environment we're in. This personality comes through most often when there is no stress. It is this part of your mind you have direct control over. It is the personality you use most for solving problems. For example, while the unconscious tells you you're thirsty, the conscious will decide to go get a drink. If you see there is juice in the fridge, you will use the conscious part of your brain to decide if you'd rather have juice or water.

The conscious personality was more fully developed in your pubescent and early adult years as you gradually separated emotionally from your guardian and began looking for acceptance with other individuals in your widening environment.

The conscious brain is active in the here and now and can project into the future by creating solutions that are original and new. It is the processor of new information. The conscious is what controls the higher cognitive functions and can think abstractly in contrast to the procedural or behavioral thinking of the unconscious and subconscious. Also, the conscious is much slower than the subconscious to answer a question, because the subconscious is repeating stored information while the conscious is creating a new answer. In a computer sense, the unconscious and subconscious are like the information stored in RAM and hard disk memory, always there ready to be accessed, while the conscious mind is like running algorithms and programs to make decisions and be creative.

This natural part of your thinking style is the one you use while playing and having fun. It is commonly used when your energy is high and you love the project or activity you are doing.

Recognizing Your Talents

If you choose to go through the process of creating your Personal Identity Profile, you will have a good grasp of your three different personal identities. If you don't choose to create your Identity Profile at this time, at least you will still have a better understanding of where your personality traits come from and a rough idea of your overall personal identity for your unconscious mind. It should be mentioned again, however, that the better you know yourself, the greater your chances for success. So now what? What are you supposed to do with this information?

Take time to recognize your talents. Based on your personalities, what do you naturally do well? When you know what your talents are, you can manage your life more effectively and focus on the things that create safety in your life. You can begin playing the game of life with rewarding results. When you try playing the game without knowing what creates safety in your personalities, you can easily get stuck and frustrated, resulting in little emotional and/or financial reward.

By playing to who you really are, you create more satisfaction in your life and you consistently achieve winning results. Remember that success breeds success. If you are playing on a team that wins consistently, your confidence increases resulting in even more wins. The same is true in the opposite direction. If you are consistently losing, your lack of confidence will continue to manifest diminishing results.

By knowing yourself and playing the game of life the way you are designed to play it, you will learn how to manage your life and get the maximum results from your efforts. When you can get all three levels of consciousness working toward the same goal in a state of love and abundance, you really are experiencing the SuperConscious and magic and miracles are created. This is how you really tap into your internal superhero.

Stop Here

This book entitles you to a free identity profile. Take the test now. Go to www.mysuccessfullife.com/identityprofile and use the pass code: kryptonitefactor. This test will give you a better understanding about your innate mind or personality.

To Thine Own Self Be True
(Week 1 Reading Assignment)

Take the test, read and re-read your personality profile each day to start to recognize your strengths.

If you are serious about changing the way you think about life and about yourself, then take the test. Study the results and begin to learn who you are and what's the core makeup of your mind, body and spirit. Many people have some anxiety or deeper fear about taking a test that potentially will disclose something they don't want to know. Here is a promise to you: no one who takes this test and really gets to know themselves lives anymore with that fear. The fear turns to love and appreciation for their unique talents and innate gifts.

If you do take the test, then you can substitute your results for the rest of this chapter. However, you may want to come back to this chapter for more ideas on how to do your emotional hygiene, which will help you maintain emotional balance and keep you in a state of abundance and love. Go ahead, take the test!

Magnitude of Thinking Style

Everyone shows a certain amount of tendencies in each thinking style; however, the styles you will want to pay the most attention to are the ones that are dominant in your profile. If you have less than 25%, then there are some tendencies, but they are not significant. If you have between 25% to 35% in any color, then these are significant and will impact your thinking and your emotions. If you have more than 35% in any thinking style, this will be your dominant thinking style in whichever mind it shows up.

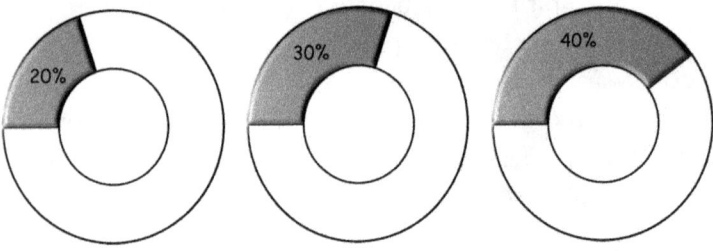

Brain Quadrants

This chapter will give you a quick overview of different personality traits; however, it will not

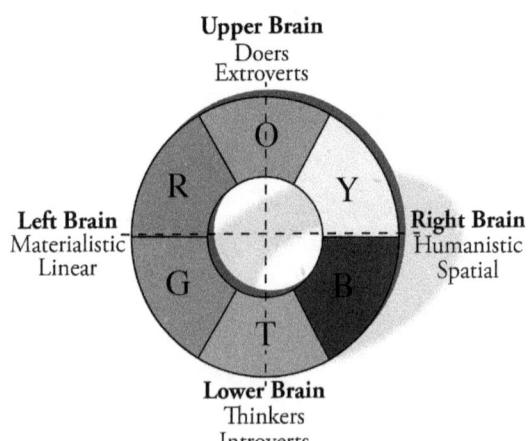

give you a detailed explanation of your different personality levels. To get your personal profile, please go to www.winningpersonality.com and follow the links to answer the questions that will generate your profile.

The brain can be divided into four sections, in theory, to help explain brain activity and dominant thinking styles. These four sections of the brain coordinate with the descriptors of the color wheel.

The left side of the brain is concrete in thinking; it wants measurements and facts. It is more linear in thinking. It has a standard of looking in the past to solve problems and mostly thinks about tangible events and items. These characteristics are often thought of as more male characteristics, because more males are left-brain dominant.

The right side of the brain is spatial in thinking; it likes creating new ideas. It likes to think about the future. It also likes to solve problems for people and with people. Many of the right-brain characteristics are thought of as being more female in nature because more females are right-brain dominant. However, we each possess attributes from both sides of the brain and our lives will change dramatically, if we learn to use both sides together in harmony.

The lower side of the brain is introspective and likes to nurture others. It can process information very quickly, causing physical responses to be slow, because many thoughts are going on at the same time.

The upper side of the brain is extroverted and likes to be physically active to solve problems. It also causes us to act quickly, sometimes before thinking, and it is more competitive with a "survival of the fittest" mentality.

Thinking Styles at a Glance – Understanding Your Powers

The following color wheel provides a brief explanation of the characteristics and traits most common in personalities with the associated identity descriptor.

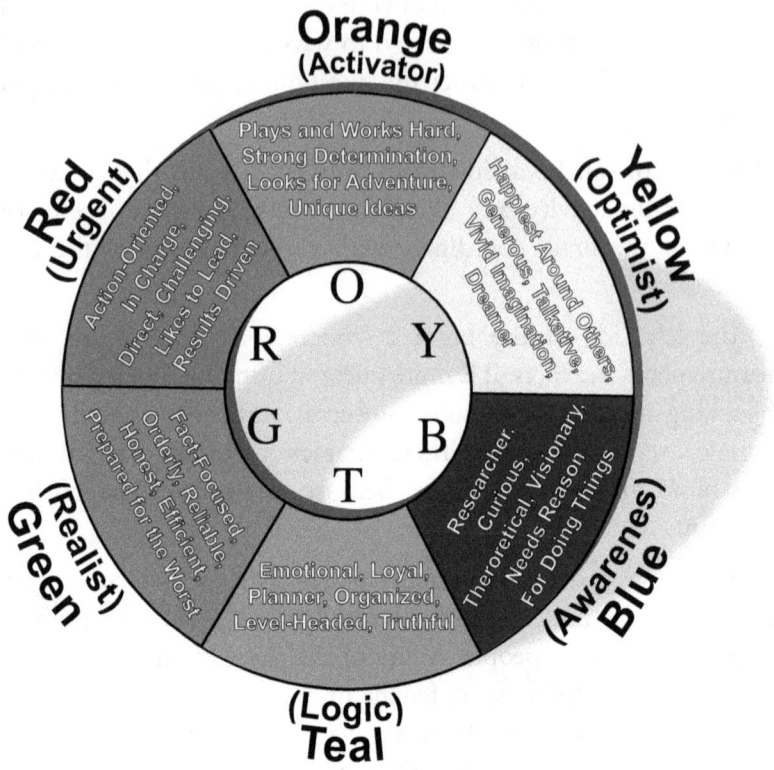

What follows is a simple description and outline of the key characteristics of each personality type and how they might react both out of fear and scarcity or abundance and love. Each personality is listed with the traits and characteristics in each of the levels of the mind when a person is feeling safe or in a state of abundance. Personality characteristics are also listed when the person is feeling unsafe or in a state of scarcity or fear. Although each personality may be described by a gender, remember that there are plenty of women who are left-brained and plenty of men who are right-brained.

Red – Urgent

Feeling Love, Abundance and Safety - Living Like a Superhero

Red personalities are left-brained people. A word that Red people associate with is loyalty in much the same way a foxhole buddy in a war thinks of loyalty. The idea of 'you cover my back and I'll cover yours.' Loyalty has to do with what you DO for the Red person. Many Red people will feel trust toward others, if they are working side-by-side with them through the good and bad times.

When a Red person is feeling safe, confident and in abundance, he will exhibit many of the following characteristics:

- Courageous
- Continual feeling of urgency – get things done – needs a To Do list
- Active in the home environment and enjoys physical tasks such as cleaning the house, sweeping the garage, or working in the garden
- Needs to be independent and in charge of things with a clear understanding of what the desired outcome and results are and wants to see everyone working toward the completion of the task
- When thinking of the past, prefers to talk about the activities and accomplishments
- Hard worker with a drive that most cannot keep up with
- Needs action and adventure
- Anything can be done and nothing is impossible
- Enjoys aggressive competition and extreme sports – they like to win, or they have to be right!

Feeling Fear, Unsafe or Scarcity – Feeling the Effects of Your Personal Kryptonite

When a Red is feeling unsafe or in scarcity, it is usually due to a break in trust with people around them. The Red person just wants results and he will take immediate action to get results. A few of the characteristics of a Red person who is feeling unsafe or scarcity include the following:

- Gets angry when things don't get done or whenever they can't seem to reach their goals – once they blow up, they recover quickly
- Uses very little tact in their relationships
- Often steps on people's feelings and doesn't care, unless it is specifically pointed out to them – gets angry when orders or directions are not followed
- Can act like a caveman and can be very brutal – most violent criminals have a lot of Red in their innate personalities
- Has to be right. "It's my way or the highway!" Must have the last word and gets angry the quickest, so arguments don't last very long

Emotional Hygiene – Replenishing Your Powers

Red personalities need to have physical action in their lives. If they will take time to do something very physical or something that involves speed like riding a bike, motorcycle or racing, they will feel much better about life. And if there is an element of danger, all the better for the Red person. The Red person needs to "blow off some steam" to balance their emotions and if they don't get some kind of physical activity, they will get angry and quick tempered more often. Here are a few activities that may serve as emotional hygiene for Red people:

- Extreme sports
- Biking, hiking, running
- Speed sports – skiing or snowboarding, racing, water sports

- Golfing, racquetball, tennis (anything that takes concentration such as hitting a ball)
- Boxing or aggressive style of martial arts
- Rigorous workouts
- If they listen to music, it should have a good beat that makes people want to move or dance

Orange – Activator

Feeling Love, Abundance and Safety - Living Like a Superhero

Orange personalities use both the left and right brains simultaneously (half Red and half Yellow) in their thinking and emotions. A word that resonates with Orange individuals is integrity. Integrity in doing what you say you're going to do. Orange people will often be organizing or directing people in ways to implement ideas. When an Orange person is feeling safe, confident and in abundance, he will exhibit many of the following characteristics:

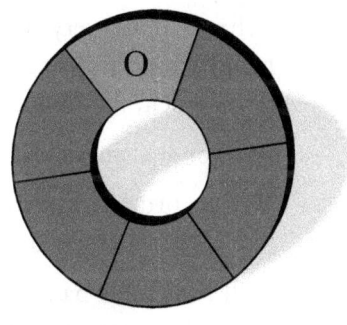

- Organizes and leads action-oriented activities that include a lot of people – catalyst for helping things get done quicker
- Good at multi-tasking
- Loves creating bigger, faster, more creative solutions to any of life's problems
- Enjoys relationships that are high-energy driven and uncomplicated
- Engages in everything with lots of enthusiasm and is confident in leading activities and selling people
- Likes people to be fully committed to a project and gets others in motion by any means possible – encouraging, pushing, or driving

- Enjoys extreme adventure, but only with a group – but tends to lose interest quickly
- Listens to different types of music, which are often upbeat
- Knows how to do just about anything and how to get others to do it, too
- Likes to be influencing and direct in all conversations – rejection doesn't bother them; instead it can fuel them

Feeling Fear, Unsafe or Scarcity – Feeling The Effects of Your Personal Kryptonite

Because an Orange person uses both his left and right brains, he can easily get stuck when he sees that he will offend someone by driving hard for the results he seeks. An Orange person has a more difficult time trusting God, the Universe and others, because he often sees so much lack of integrity in people and in the world at large.

- Caught or stuck in the challenge of getting things done but still being accepted
- Believes that everything he does is wrong and he starts to believe that this fear is normal – every time he gets something done quick, it feels like he hurt someone's feelings
- Feels or acts angry all the time
- Will be brutally forceful, beating people up verbally, yet feels like it's just part of an average day
- Will justify his bad feelings by saying to himself, "I'm going to do this now and I know I'm going to make enemies, but if that's what I'm going to have to do to succeed, I'll do it!"

Emotional Hygiene – Replenishing Your Powers

Orange people need to be actively engaged in multiple activities with people. Orange people like to do exciting things but like activities to be new and varied. Where a Red person can go do the same high-energy activity over and over again, the Orange person needs to change things up and be in charge of the fun. Some of the activities that can help clear away negative emotions include:

- Arranging a family outing
- Spur of the moment group activities – planning a quick trip to take a hike or go camping
- Organizing groups or group activities
- Exciting things like parachuting with some buddies
- Researching new ideas
- Building something new that requires help from others
- Organizing humanitarian efforts
- Team sports – basketball, soccer, volleyball, football, baseball or softball

Yellow – Optimist

Feeling Love, Abundance and Safety - Living Like a Superhero

Yellow people are right-brained people. A word that describes Yellow is acceptance. Yellow people will do anything, including 'giving you the shirt off their back' to gain your acceptance. The Yellow person's acceptance is more about who they are than what they do. Here are a few characteristics a Yellow would have or experience:

- True 'people person' who can enjoy the company of a single individual or a group
- Generous and an optimist who needs being with and around people at all times
- Likes to make others laugh and be the life of the party and will often do things in an unpredictable way

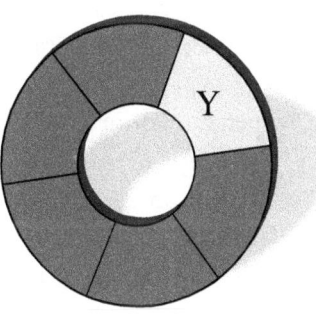

- Loves to be a host and entertain guests and is always looking for fun and entertaining things to do
- Strong desire to be friends with everyone and will help people out to increase her popularity and acceptance – goes along with whatever the group decides to do
- Will often be late to events or on projects – committed to doing too many things (can't say 'no') at one time and often talks too long
- Expands the truth in her conversations in order to seek approval and loves to drop names in order to impress people
- Social rules mean nothing and will often get in trouble, but she can talk herself out of most altercations – will break the rules to impress or help others
- Loud, happy, upbeat, and very chatty – loves to hear the sound of her own voice – and is well versed in a wide range of topics, so she can carry a conversation with anyone
- No limitations in communications – can approach a bum on the street or walk up to the President or Ruler of the country and have a good conversation with either of them

Feeling Fear, Unsafe or Scarcity – Feeling The Effects of Your Personal Kryptonite

It's hard to get a Yellow person down, but when she is down, she will often react in such a way that will be socially damaging. A Yellow person will let everyone know that she isn't feeling great so that she will gain sympathy. Here are a few other ways in which a Yellow person will react if she is feeling unsafe or scarcity in her life:
- Engages in gossiping and socially undermines others
- Acts from a social agenda and is very meddlesome in others' affairs
- Can wreak havoc in a social organization by divulging 'dirt' on people
- Will involve as many as she can in her complaints – "Misery loves company"
- Can whine and bellyache like no other, but when

confronted directly, she will not say much and will submit to the will of the other person

Emotional Hygiene – Replenishing Your Powers

Yellow people need to be enjoying a party or a get together. Yellow people are driven by acceptance and therefore are always looking to be a part of the group. Some of the activities that keep Yellow people feeling on top of their game include:

- Having lunch with friends
- Organizing groups or group activities
- Being the host or hostess of a party – must budget money so they can throw a regular party
- Listening to fun, upbeat music – party music or music to dance to
- Having a game night with friends or family
- Calling, texting or communicating with multiple people
- Team sports – basketball, soccer, volleyball, football, baseball or softball

Blue – Awareness

Feeling Love, Abundance and Safety - Living Like A Superhero

The Blue person, like the Red person, relates to the word of Loyalty. However, in the case of the Blue person, loyalty is more related to self and to who the person is than to other people. Being loyal and true to yourself is far more important to a Blue person than just about any other personality. Other attributes of a Blue person include the following:

- Seeks and acquires great wisdom, awareness, and spirituality
- Feels a deep love and connectedness to everything and everyone and enjoys

hugging others and being hugged – she can forgive but has a hard time forgetting because of the great depth that she feels love and pain

- Very intuitive, sensitive, and emotional, romantic, nature lover and loyal to a cause
- Enjoys deep thinking conversations about love, art, or the purpose of life and needs more down time to regenerate, meditate, and feel good emotionally
- Needs to be creative, doing something artistic or playing musical instruments
- Enjoys gaining a deep awareness in specialized subjects and sharing her wisdom and is good at teaching or preaching information or advocating a cause to others – can sit and think all day and not believe it's a waste of time
- Likes to be a problem solver and is recognized for having the wisdom to create the solution – often tinkers with ideas, designs, functionality and solutions
- Wears her emotions on her sleeves and wants to be loved for who she is, not what she does – loves being viewed as unique and special
- Likes smaller, more intimate relationships with friends and will openly share deep feelings
- Likes to help find solutions to emotional issues and can often give advice to others about their personal lives, but she has a challenge seeing or defining her own problems
- Is a very nurturing person and likes to be nurtured

Feeling Fear, Unsafe or Scarcity – Feeling The Effects of Your Personal Kryptonite

A Blue person feels her emotions deeper than anyone else, so when she is feeling 'Blue,' she is feeling deep pain and emotional disparity. The people who get the most depressed are often the Blue people. Other emotions and characteristics a Blue person will exhibit include the following:

- Can be very moody, withdrawn or very depressed and may think about suicide more than any other personality
- Will push the social norms and engage in what others think of as masochistic behaviors and put up walls and barriers that require significant effort to get to know them
- Will continually think about and rehash conversations or social episodes where she wishes she had said or done something differently
- Have to be right, they want the last word, but they can argue their point for weeks or months in order to get the last word

Emotional Hygiene – Replenishing Your Powers

Blue people are deep thinkers and need time to sort through their thoughts and emotions. Blue people also need to have a 9-1-1 friend with whom they can call and discuss anything. Some of the activities that Blue people use to feel secure and safe include:

- Reading or writing
- Creative activities – either by hand or on computer – painting, photography, cooking, crafts that can be customized or observing someone else's art
- Meditation or prayer
- Spending time connecting with nature – doing something in water or taking time to appreciate beauty in nature
- Yoga, flowing martial arts, or some form of physical activity where they are always learning or testing themselves
- Listening to music that has a meaning – words or feeling to music
- Conversing about 'deeper' subjects of learning, self-awareness or spirituality

- Doing some kind of process of alternative healing or self-healing
- Some learning activity – either in a group or by self

Teal – Logic

Feeling Love, Abundance and Safety - Living Like A Superhero

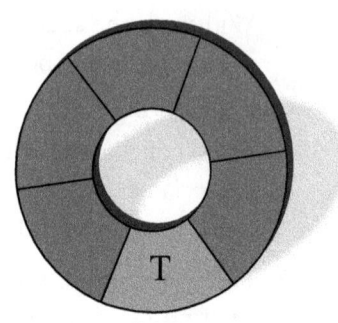

Like the Orange, Teal people relate strongly to the concept of integrity. However, the integrity is more directed inward than outward. She is much more driven by processes and the integrity of a process and she is always looking for the perfect or optimal process.

- Prudent, logical, and does not mind being alone and often enjoys it
- Family unit is usually close knit and will very seldom create a commotion, as she desires no conflict in the relationship
- Will often have an unorganized personal space, as she prefers being involved in thinking rather than actively doing things
- Spiritual protectors – she looks inside to solve problems and will figure out a way to send a prayer or kind thought toward others – has the ability to hold everyone in a safe place
- Deepest of thinkers and problem solvers, constantly looking for facts and figures along with inspiration and new ideas
- Finds satisfaction in being recognized for her ability to do the right things for the right reasons, sacrificing for the higher good
- Master of recognizing other's feelings
- Always acts with logic – both emotional logic and systematic logic – always looking for the optimal or perfect solution

- Likes to be in deep thought and prefers complex problems to analyze
- Can both think up an idea and figure out the best method to implement a plan to manage toward success
- She is commonly quiet and takes very pragmatic action

Feeling Fear, Unsafe or Scarcity – Feeling The Effects of Your Personal Kryptonite

The Teal person who is feeling unsafe or scarcity will often question everything she thinks and does and wonder if there is something wrong with her. She will also be paralyzed more than other personalities because she can't measure the results of emotions. The following are a few more of the characteristics of a Teal person who is feeling unsafe or insecure:

- Will think, 'Everything I do is wrong!"
- Won't want to act without emotion, yet she can't measure what she feels, so she goes back and forth between, "I want to feel that it's right, but I want to make sure (measure) that it's right"
- If there isn't any logic, then she can't act – It's either logical or it's unsafe and she will become defensive until logic lines up in her mind
- Emotions of being defensive can cascade to other events/projects in her life
- Can become very depressed and will become despondent and won't talk

Emotional Hygiene – Replenishing Your Powers

Teal people are among the deepest logical thinkers and need ways to express their thoughts. Teal people need to be working through processes to find the optimal results. Teals are at their best when doing activities such as:

- Writing in a journal or writing thoughtful letters or emails to people

- Meditation or prayer
- Listening to or playing soothing, peaceful music
- Spending time connecting to nature – doing something around water
- Conversing with others to express logic about situations and solutions
- Creating new things with their hands – doesn't need to follow a set process
- Listening to water – such as a fountain or waterfall
- Reorganizing things – coming up with a better way of doing things in the home or in a business

Green – Realist

Feeling Love, Abundance and Safety - Living Like A Superhero

There isn't a more polite person to be around than a Green who is feeling abundant. Acceptance for what he does or provides for others is part of the Green person's needs. Green people will often accept responsibility without thinking about it, because he wants to do things to gain recognition and acceptance.

- Likes having safe, simple, structured, predictable, no hype environments
- Will commonly have a schedule posted on the fridge, in the den, and maybe even in the bathroom – time is a big measuring device

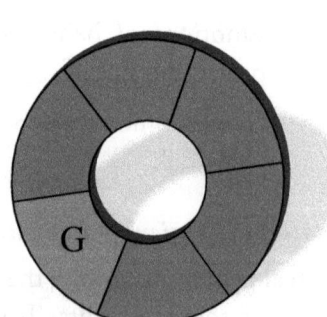

- Enjoys boundaries and rules in life and communicates safety all the time and will plan ahead to resolve any difficulties
- Has a better concept of what is right and wrong than any other personalties – "When in doubt, choose the safest route"

and won't associate or hang around destructive or disruptive people
- Gains respect by being very reliable, consistent, and by doing things right
- He finds safety in rules and detailed guidelines, because of the desire for a measurable outcome – wants everyone to follow the rules so everything is fair
- Very polite and proper in his demeanor and known for his patience – is very friendly when asked questions or when a conversation is initiated and moved along by another person
- Enjoys a wide range of activities as long as the activity has established rules or guidelines and likes to return to things he enjoys, like games, locations, vacations, and activities – very good at winning by the rules of any game
- Peacemakers and peacekeepers and are almost always friendly and ready to help the greater good of the group
- Likes doing something constructive when he feels good, but is more about task-oriented things that aren't high energy, which allows him to think more

Feeling Fear, Unsafe or Scarcity – Feeling The Effects of Your Personal Kryptonite

The Green person who is feeling unsafe or scarcity looks more and more to the rules to find safety and will evaluate life based on whether or not it is 'fair'. Because the Green person can see so much detail, he will constantly be pointing out what is wrong, unfair, or problematic. The following details more about the Green person who feels unsafe:

- Pessimistic, where everything is wrong, nitpicker and legalistic about every thing – tears himself and others down
- Has a major talent for justifying everything and often tortures himself with justification in an unjust world and can torture himself into depression
- Always thinks there is something wrong with him

- Can develop fear about everything, because there is no justice around – "Nothing is fair!" – and will stop talking and become very quite and personally withdrawn
- Won't talk, but won't leave a conflict either – will stare at you with indignity and not answer any questions, because words have a definite meaning and will become conflicted with semantics and choose not to speak, because whatever is said might be turned against him
- Can forgive, but finds it hard to forget

Emotional Hygiene – Replenishing Your Powers

Green people plain and simply need to follow a process. A Green Person's activities could include:

- Doing something with hands – knitting, crocheting or doing puzzles
- Playing a musical instrument
- Listening to or playing soothing, peaceful music
- Following a recipe while cooking
- Playing games with patterns – board games or card games
- Doing a 'Green Thumb' activity like yard work or working in a garden
- Doing their finances or something where numbers add up
- Sorting or organizing things – doing house work, cleaning up a room, organizing a closet or work area

Combinations and Opposites:

There are a few more personality combinations to consider. What's listed is more of the positive aspects of these personality mixes; however, in most cases scarcity and fear bring out mostly the opposite emotions and behaviors. Many sabotaging emotions come from the second largest personality in the Unconscious mind or Innate mind, because it often leads to mixed emotions and fear. If the person can trust himself or herself and others with the second strongest personality trait, they can begin to experience the stronger personality in full.

Here are a few combinations and opposites that should be noted:

Red/Blue   (Maverick) –
Individualistic and entrepreneurial in his approach. These individuals can come up with several different ideas and take immediate action to see which works best. He is very driven, but has a hard time allowing people to work for him, because in his mind, his way is the best way. He can outthink most and outdo the rest. He

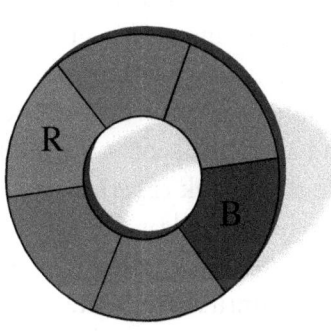

has strong ties to loyalty to self, to a cause, or to people who work hard at his side. When feeling unsafe, this person will become more and more individualistic in his approach, not caring about what anyone thinks or feels about him.

Green/Yellow (Cooperative Guru) – Group and organizational oriented. Knows and follows the rules and help others do the same. She is very good at motivating others to follow processes. This person does very well in middle management within corporations, especially in process-driven, larger corporations. She can organize people and activities and she works well with everyone. This person is very adept at working within organizations and is naturally

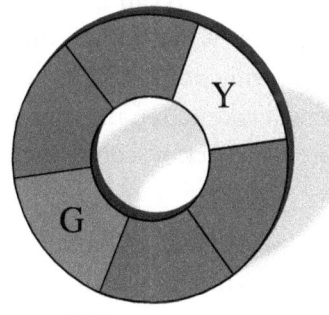

gifted in political affairs. When feeling unsafe, this person will go along with the group, but always cover her bases, documenting all the problems and the reasons why her original ideas and rules were better than the group's.

Yellow/Blue (Right-Brained) – Delves into the intangible and motivated by feelings. These individuals can find many solutions, get others involved in the solutions and then coordinate efforts to get it done. She feels best working in groups of people who come up with new ideas and share their ideas freely. She likes the think tank experience, where she can bounce ideas off other people. When feeling unsafe, this person will not act until she feels safe emotionally.

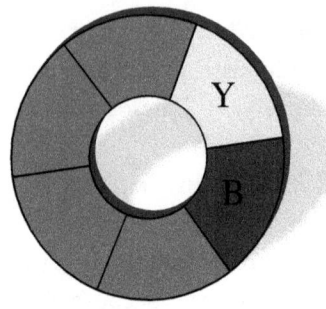

Red/Green (Left-Brained) – Driven by tangible results and task oriented. These individuals can organize and then take immediate action. If he discovers a process that works, he will work it to death, which will often make him very financially successful. The Red/Green person is very active, who can think and refine as he goes. When feeling unsafe, this person will continue to look for logic and will take action in order to gather more data. Action comes before the emotion.

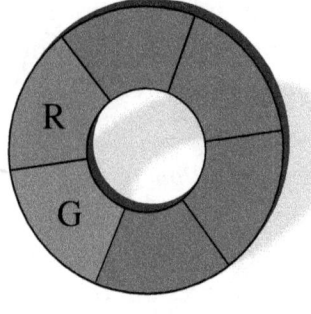

Orange/Teal (Chameleon) – Can feel great about doing just about anything, which often leads this person to wonder what he should be doing. Can emotionally connect with many different people. Is often passionate about creating harmony, peace or equity in life. When in his element and feeling secure, this

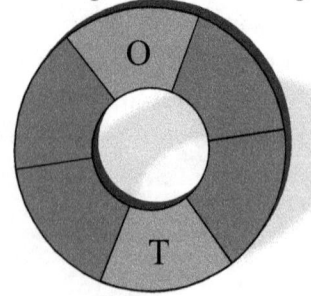

person can see the optimal solution and convince others that it is the right solution for them. When feeling unsafe, this person will think that everything is wrong about himself and that nothing he does or thinks or feels is right.

Making It Crystal Clear

1) In order to know your strengths, you must understand yourself and the way you think.

2) You have three levels of consciousness or awareness; Conscious (Intending) mind, Subconscious (Imprinted) mind and Unconscious (Innate) mind.

3) Personality traits are manifested by whether you utilize your left-brain or right-brain more or if you use both simultaneously.

4) There are six colors that represent the different personality traits and each of these six are found in all three levels of consciousness; Red, Orange, Yellow, Blue, Teal and Green.

Intentional Vision Exercises

1) Share at least three wins you had this week with someone close to you.

2) Go online to take the complete Personal Identity Profile. Read through the results each day for five days – write down notes about connections you make during the week with your Personal Identity Profile report.

3) Observe your actions each day and compare your feelings with the Personal Identity Profile. Do your best to compare your subconscious programs with your unconscious feelings. Keep journal notes.

Chapter 3

Trusting Life By
Trusting God And The Universe

Your mind is not only the most powerful co-creation tool, but it was also built to protect you from pain. Somewhere your kryptonite became evident when you experienced enough pain to fall out of trust with life. That's when your subconscious mind kicked in and created a pattern that protects you from similar experiences. The only problem is that it protects you from anything that it thinks might cause you pain. For example, if at some point your parent yelled at you when you were a small kid, "You can't do anything right, can you?" and you felt the pain deep enough, you may always be playing a pattern in your mind about how you're not good enough. Another example is if you were doing your very best at something and someone laughed and mocked what you were doing. Now you hold back because something inside your head says that people will not appreciate your efforts. In other words, you lost trust with yourself in that experience and you continue to run that same pattern, but it shows up in many different scenarios.

Love, especially self-love, is founded in trust.

This Intentional Vision process of finding your major weakness will help improve your life, both professionally and personally. But we must point out, it can only change your life if you are willing to change. It will take an inner desire to be the best you can be and a commitment to yourself to listen for meaning, ask questions for understanding, and be proactive with all the exercises.

It takes trust to believe you are in the right place at the right time; that you have what it takes to become your full potential and that your underlying desires to be the standard for leadership and success at any level is achievable. It is time to become yourself and live life large.

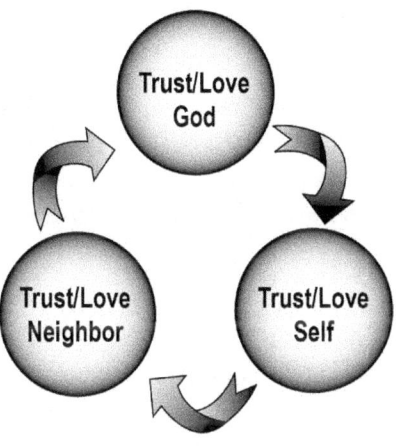

Trust is the key to finding and experiencing love in your life. You could love God but be self-deprecating and still not experience true love. You could have a feeling of confidence in yourself and your abilities but not trust the actions and intentions of others and still not feel a deep sense of connection and love. It takes trust in three key areas – Life (through a higher power or source), Self and Others as illustrated above.

The 1st Law of Intentional Vision – Trust Life And That God and the Universe Hold a Higher Purpose For You
(Week 2 Reading Assignment)

Superman turned to images and lessons from his real father to understand who he was and the purpose and reason for his powers. The same is true for you. You must rely on a power greater than you, no matter how you might define that power, and then trust that you are here for a reason. Then look for the reason every day.

Trusting the Universe is the foundation of all success, it's truly the first step to acquiring the freedom to do or be anything you want. The simple fact is, that before you attempt anything, you must trust or have a belief that the outcome is possible.

For example, if you don't trust that the grocery store will have a loaf of bread, you'll not even attempt to go get one. It is the same with anything; if you don't trust the Universe will supply your needs you won't go get whatever it is you are in need of. Without trust, any effort you put forth is going to be shallow and insignificant.

Trust is a key element that must be learned in order to create the results you want in life. If you do not trust the power and potential of the Universe, you will not be able to overcome some of the simple obstacles that might stand in your way. It is very difficult to put forth a true effort if you have doubt in the outcome.

Trust is truly the foundation needed to make changes in your life. Trust the Universe and know that it has everything you will ever need or want. Those who don't trust the Universe will barely have the necessities of life. In fact, they will find themselves to be underemployed, in excessive debt, or in unhealthy relationships. And to compound the issue, they lack the level of trust needed to change their life just enough to get the ball rolling.

Most people halfheartedly try to achieve success; but in reality they have already accepted failure before they even start. They do this because they lack trust in the Universe. They don't believe the Universe will give them what they want. They don't believe they will get an honest day's pay for an honest effort.

I know you have tried things and failed...but I also know that if you learn from what the Universe is teaching you and trust that the Universe wants to help you achieve your goals, your continued efforts will produce results. The true power and potential that you possess is unlimited, but it is commonly reduced to a shadow of your potential because of not trusting the Universe – not believing you will be compensated for your efforts.

I know many people have had things happen in their life that seem unfair, or unjust. And because the pain of the unfairness is a dominant thought, most of them completely lose trust with the Universe. If you believe that there is fair and equitable exchange in the Universe – a level of trust where you know you deserve what you want – the Universe will always provide.

When there is trust in the Universe, a force will well up inside you. You'll have an inner faith, an innate belief, which will allow you to place enormous confidence in a safe outcome. This same force, this indescribable feeling, is used often by the most successful people in the world. However, you will only access this feeling, or force, when you begin to trust the Universe.

When you trust the outcome, you will change your life, your economics, your safety, and your peace. It all comes through trust. The amount of physical energy you are willing to put forth is in direct proportion to the level of trust you have in the Universe. The first step, however, is that you trust the Universe will provide what it is you desire.

And those that trust the most do the most to succeed – they take the most action. They really pull themselves up by their bootstraps and engage in obtaining their desires. They learn and strive for success, and in the end they find that real success is understanding who they really are.

Everyone is looking for the feeling of internal warmth and satisfaction that 'I have what it takes,' and 'I measure up to my standards.' Everyone is born with the potential to succeed but the fear of success holds some back. Everyone falls down; everyone is learning how to be the best they can be. Yet, you can only learn how to get up by falling down and having moments of pain. It is not a punishment, there is a lesson to be learned and it is up to you to turn your mistake into wisdom.

In life, mistakes are really your friends; they are essential to the learning process. Without falling you will never learn how to pick yourself up.

The most common mistake about falling down is that people keep their attention on the falling and not the getting up. They continue to relive the same mistakes over and over again. They maintain constant negative self talk and attitudes and simply never get up.

Those that think negative thoughts do negative and get negative in return. Those that think good thoughts do good and get good in return. It is a fatal error to have negative thoughts because those thoughts turn into negative attitudes and breed fear and self-destruction (lack of trust). Those who are in a negative state will feel that an outside force is in control causing them to conform for safety, or in other words… self-sabotage (safety in failure). They become a real victim, blaming others for their choices.

By placing trust in the Universe you will be able to keep your attitude in alignment with your goals. You will avoid being a victim. You will ultimately experience the clear knowing that your thoughts become your outcome. And if you don't trust your future then a place of emptiness is waiting for you.

To win in life vicariously is sometimes sweet but that sweetness will fade quickly. When you are playing to win, you will accumulate your victories as a self-made, self-agent experiencing freedom. And that is the ultimate win.

When you discover that the foundation for gaining freedom is to trust the Universe, you'll quickly understand that true success is a privilege that is learned and earned. It is up to each individual to experience their spiritual journey towards accomplishing their goals… and I know you will accomplish yours!

So remember that any exchange in life takes trust, to be successful in business takes trust, to have successful relationships takes trust, and to enjoy time you have in life takes trust.

It takes trust to believe that the Universe is always in fair exchange. Trusting that the Universe is giving you exactly what you are asking for at a spiritual level takes trust. It takes trust to know there are no accidents and that life is all about miracles and there are no mistakes.

The birds that gather worms need trust, they trust that they will find the food and bring it back each day. And the phrase, "The early bird gets the worm," is still true and so is the phrase "God helps those that help themselves."

Trust the Universe is waiting for you to help yourself. Start right now by trusting that the Universe wants you to have the biggest business deals, be in the best relationships, and spend your time in pleasure. You will find the Universe will always give you more opportunities than you thought possible. Without action, trust is a false hope; but action with trust is the seed of success. A major key to achieving anything you want is to trust at such a level that action happens at an instinctive level; at a level that you engage with full energy and passion.

Just like the bird that leaves its nest in the morning to gather food, it simply acts out of instinct and so will you when you regain your ability to trust the Universe at the level you were designed to.

> Let go and let God by trusting that the Universe is waiting for your action because the Universe already knows what you want. It is just waiting for you to know what you want and to take action. And when you do, the Universe will respond because the law of fair exchange is always in place.

Rude Awakening

> *Our best-built certainties are but sand-houses and subject to damage from any wind of doubt that blows.*
> – Mark Twain, "The Great Dark"

I continue to be amazed at how God or the Universe continues to show up in amazing ways in my life and it happens every time I believe it will or when I simply let go and let God. I'm just an ordinary guy. Like many of you, I'm married, I have kids, I live in middle-class America and I have dreams of becoming something more in my life. And because I believe that the Universe is there to help me, I'm also one who will take a chance and go for it to try and make my life better.

I was doing fairly well in the technology industry. I was well liked in my work group and I was making a name for myself within my department. But then the dot com era came along and there were so many people moving around trying to get the best deal that would make them millionaires. I was offered a position in an e-Learning company with the potential to make millions. I took it and pursued the dream. But like many others, the dream evaporated when I was laid off before I could realize any profits from my work.

As we neared Christmas that year, there was a great feeling of excitement around the company that everyone would soon be a wealthy owner of a new future in technology. I had 40,000 stock options at $3.50 each. A similar e-Learning company had recently gone public and was selling for around $30 a share. Another e-Learning company was selling in the $40 range. I would be able to exercise the first third of my options on my first year anniversary in a few months, which was about the time the company was projecting to go public. Over the next couple of years, I expected to make between $500,000 to $1.5 million or more from my stock options.

To add fuel to everyone's fire, the e-Learning company I worked for had its yearly Christmas party on a Friday, early in December, in a new banquet room near one of the newest and most prestigious golf courses in the area. It was a festive occasion with plenty of presents and a great feeling of abundance. I won a couple of nice presents in a gift swap game. The new President was announced at the end of the Christmas party. Along with the announcement, there had been a presentation about the new organizations within the company. There were two organizations I could easily fit into; however, my name wasn't on the chart. "There must be a mistake," I thought. "Maybe they just want to know which group I want to work in?" I thought to myself.

The following Monday, both the new Vice President of Marketing and the Vice President of Product Management spoke to me and they both wanted me on their team. Now it looked like it came down to my choice. Would I go with my strengths and stay in the Marketing arena or would I choose to continue learning new skills and grow in another well sought after profession in the hi-tech workplace? I enjoyed working with the Product Management Vice President, who had brought me into the company, but many people had realized my talents in marketing. I even appeared on a previous organization chart as the Marketing Director. It was a tough decision. A decision I would never have to make.

I arrived early Tuesday morning at the office to finish compiling a list of all my projects and the status of each. The e-Learning company I worked for was on the brink of going public and there had been some restructuring in the management to prepare for a move to Wall Street. The new President, a man who I had helped gain greater favor with the largest Internet Service Providers in the world by creating visionary reports on the e-Learning industry, had asked me to come in and meet with him. This hopefully would mean a move up in the organization.

It was 8 a.m. and it was time to take my folder of projects and go meet with the new President. The blinds were pulled on the windows of the "fish bowl" conference room. I turned the corner, smiled and opened the door. Inside the room sat three people, the new President, the man who was the company's legal council, and the HR representative. I immediately wanted to turn around and go back to my desk. My heart sank into my stomach as I scanned the three somber faces. The new President said, "Have a seat, Adam," and said nothing else.

The HR representative spoke with tension in her voice; "Adam as of this morning your employment here is being terminated. This is part of a restructuring we're going through…" My mind checked out for a moment as she went through some of the details. I felt as if someone had hit me first in the stomach and then in the head. The fog wasn't quite clear and I almost felt as if I were a third party looking in on this ridiculous scene.

"What a fool I was!" I screamed inside my head. "To think I did everything I could to help this company. Two Vice Presidents want me on their teams and now I'm being let go! I don't get it?"

"Adam, you will receive a one month's severance, once you have signed the document that indicates you won't take any legal action against this company," the HR representative continued. "You will have 15 days to sign the document or you will forfeit your severance…"

"There's got to be a mistake," I thought. I was still immobilized by this surreal experience. "What am I going to tell my wife?" I thought as the weight of the event sank me lower into my chair.

"Are there any questions?" the HR representative asked.

I turned to face the new President and I simply asked, "Why?"

The President replied, "You've done great work for us, so I want to thank you for that. But…we are changing a few things around here and we don't see a need for you in the organization. That's all there is to say." He stared at me with an empty expression on his face. The new President was right, there wasn't anything else to say. I stood up and anger rose in my body like the blood rushing back to my face. I clinched my fist, hesitated, then reached for the door, and walked out.

The HR representative escorted me back to my desk. I entered the office and shared what had just happened with my two friends and coworkers. People started to gather around. "What happened? What's going on?" asked my office mates.

"I don't know. All I know is that they are laying me off," I said, anger building in my voice. A box was placed on my desk. I politely thanked the person and continued, "I don't know why, except that it seems to be political."

"Who's letting you go? Is anyone else getting laid off?"

"I don't know about anyone else. It's strange that two Vice Presidents want me, and yet, I seem to be the only one that's getting laid off!" I packed up my desk, taking my time to place everything in the box. I wanted to deny what was happening to me, maybe if I dragged it out, someone would come in and say I could stay.

I erased all the projects that were outlined on the white board, wanting to erase everything I'd done for the company. I turned to my office mates and said, "I should have known something was up when he (the new President) came in yesterday and asked you all sorts of questions about the idea that was essentially mine. It was almost as if I wasn't there. The only time he acknowledged that I was in the room was when he turned around and said he wanted to see me in his office this morning."

One of my office mates said, "Yeah that was strange. I was trying to figure out why he just didn't ask you about that idea. It was yours and you were standing right there."

I was now locked out of my computer and couldn't retrieve any of the files I wanted. I wanted some of the documents to add to my portfolio of accomplishments. The feelings of being a failure were setting in. The only thing that bolstered me was that everyone was as shocked as I was.

I had been a rising star in my ability to come up with new and original ideas. I had put together business proposals that had turned heads with large potential customers. I had put together advertising plans and budgets. I had been called in to save the day and bring more life to the business plan, which the company paid a lot of money to develop. The business plan was one of the key deliverables to the high-powered brokerage firm that was taking the e-Learning company public. Now I was being escorted from the building with nothing more than a cardboard box full of my personal effects.

"I just got laid off," I told my wife as I sat in my cold car. "I don't know why. All I can think is that it's political. It has to be either the new President or the new Vice President of Marketing." I sat still, head laid back, wanting to cry, but an emptiness filled my chest. A long pause in the conversation – nothing more needed to be said. "I'll be home in twenty minutes… I'm sitting in my car now… I love you."

Being laid off like that left me in shock, wondering if I was living someone else's life. In a way I was living someone else's life and at that moment, it was time to find my purpose in my new experience in life.

Because you're reading this, I've accomplished the goals along my journey that started when I was laid off from that e-Learning company. At this point in my life, I can look back and say that the experience of being laid off was meant to be. There isn't anything other than that sudden change in career that could have taught me the lessons or helped me meet the people I needed in my life in order to reach my current goals and destiny.

I look back now over every position I've ever had and it seems that things just fell into place so I could be there at that point in time. Each job brought me closer to today, helping me learn the lessons I needed and giving me the skills and experience to face this day with passion and enthusiasm. However, that awareness hasn't always been there and I've often felt trapped by my circumstances. I often felt like there should be more to life – but what?

Why is Superman always in the right place to save people? Because he was supposed to be there. You are no different. If you were supposed to be somewhere else, learning different lessons or making a difference in another way, then you'd be there instead of where you are right now.

The Eagle Who Thought He Was A Chicken

*We ought to fly away from earth to heaven as quickly as we can; and to
fly away is to become like God, as far as this is possible;
and to become like him is to become holy, just, and wise.*
— Plato

My experience of living a life in the high-paced, busy corporate world, without a clearly defined purpose, often reminds me of a story I once heard in a church sermon about an eagle that once lived among chickens. Here is how I remember the story:

A farmer was hiking in the mountains near his farm. He came upon a tree with an eagle's nest. The farmer was an inquisitive fellow and decided to climb the tree to see if there was anything in the nest. He found, when he reached the top of the tree, that there were two eggs in the eagle's nest. He decided that he would take one of the eggs home and see what would happen when the eagle hatched. He grabbed an egg, stuffed it in his pocket and headed back home to his farm.

When the farmer arrived home, he realized he didn't really have any way to raise an eagle if and when the egg hatched, so he decided to put the egg out with the chickens in the chicken coop. A hen sat on the egg and soon it hatched.

The hatchling was a big bird and many of the chickens didn't know what to do about the large baby bird. Yet, the eagle imprinted on its mother hen and began to follow her around and do everything she did. The eaglet pecked at the ground like its mother hen did, it flapped its wings and strutted around like its mother hen did. The eaglet was soon doing everything a chicken would and the other chickens accepted the eaglet as one of them.

It was the rooster of the coop that first said something to the eagle, "You know, you really aren't like the rest of us. Don't get me wrong, we like having you around. All the other predators don't come around our coop because of you.

But here's the thing, you aren't a chicken, you're an eagle and you should be flying. The eagle paid very little attention to the rooster; he spotted a grasshopper on the ground and hopped off to catch it.

The farmer had watched the eagle grow with fascination. He first thought it was funny that an eagle would act like a chicken. The fascination turned into bewilderment, and then to worry. "What if that eagle always wants to be a chicken," the farmer wondered to himself. He thought, "I think it's about time to teach that eagle how to be an eagle."

So the next morning the farmer got up early and grabbed the eagle and held him high in the air and said, "You are an eagle, fly like an eagle!" The eagle saw the other chickens pecking around on the ground. The eagle flapped its wings, landed on the ground and hopped back over to where the other chickens were feeding.

The farmer decided that he needed to get the eagle up higher, so he would have a chance to flap his wings more, which would help the eagle remember that he was an eagle. The next morning, the farmer took the eagle and climbed to the top of his barn. There on the crest of the roof, the farmer lifted his arm and said, "You are a eagle, fly!" The eagle looked across the horizon and saw the tops of other barns and silos. For a moment, the farmer thought he saw something in the eagle's eyes. Maybe the eagle would remember who he really was. The eagle looked from side to side, then he looked down at the ground and saw the chickens pecking at the ground. The eagle flapped his wings and fluttered down to the ground to be close to the creatures he knew most.

This latest episode really perplexed and frustrated the farmer. How could this beautiful bird forget who he was supposed to be? The farmer realized he'd have to take a journey with the eagle, back up to the mountains, away from the farmyard environment.

The following day, the farmer arose early and took the eagle with him. He traveled back up to the mountains;

he rode on horseback up to the base of one of the tallest mountains. The farmer took the eagle on his arm and hiked the rest of the way to the top of the mountain. When he reached the peak, he held the eagle out so that the eagle could see the vast beauty that lay below. As he held the eagle out, a strong breeze surged up from below. The eagle felt the breeze, it could see for miles. The eagle stretched out its wings and took flight.

> *The future belongs to those who believe in the beauty of their dreams.*
> – Eleanor Roosevelt

I felt like an eagle that had been living with chickens. My dream was bigger than simply making money where so many people are just pecking around in the coop of my day-to-day world. I needed a way to express myself and really make a difference in my life and see the difference I was making in the lives of others. I knew I could do it, but I didn't know how. But how can you do what you want to do when you're stuck in the barnyard and there are no mountains around to see. I had to find a way, a person, who would take me to a higher place and let the cool wind blow under my wings, a place where I could see without limitations. But where do you find such a person?

In all honesty, I was afraid to take flight by myself. Part of me wanted to stay in the chicken coop, where I felt safe, and at the same time, it was the chicken coop that made me think that eventually I was going to be on the chopping block again. I'm sure there are many people who can relate to this feeling: to have dreams, but no way to reach them with any sense of safety in your life. I was looking for a farmer to take me to the mountains and help me see that I could soar.

Do you ever feel like you're not living up to your potential? How much of your thinking is related to thinking about what could have been or telling yourself that you don't deserve better? Let go of those negative beliefs and thought patterns and you'll take off.

What Does Trusting Life Mean

People choose to trust life in different ways. One way is to simply believe that life was set up in whatever way for you. For example, you might walk into a job interview and just feel like things are going to go your way. It's just an innate feeling you have that all is great and will work out for you in the end – call it your ego, call it good karma or call it good luck, but whatever it is, you know you have it.

Another way to have trust in life is to believe that you are a perfect product of a perfect universe and that you're here to act as part of that universe. Everything works together and you are a part of that greater whole, that collective conscience of the Universe. So when you don't get that job or you have something that doesn't work out as planned, you know that it will work out for your greater good and the greater good for everyone and everything.

Then there is the third way, which is to trust that a Creator or God has put you here for a reason. That reason for being here in this existence is what gives you trust. Trusting God is trusting your future. With a loving and all-knowing God, you wouldn't be here unless God meant it to be so. Oh, by the way, these ways of trusting your life are not mutually exclusive – you can trust in one, two or all three of these ways and you will find that your level of trust will dictate how much you will be able to trust yourself and others within your experience in life.

Some scientists and medical people have identified that you have a "God-spot" in your brain. This area of the brain is related to thoughts pertaining to God, spirituality and other existential emotions. Some people will use this analysis to explain why people believe in a superior being, while those who believe, will point to the fact that by divine design, you are created to believe.

Whichever way you want to look at it, you are made to trust in life or the environment in which you live. Otherwise, you would live in a constant state of fear.

Take for example some of the financial and economic problems that have taken place in the last 100 years, including the more recent ones. The true reason for the financial meltdowns is fear or lack of trust in the future. If you believe you are subject to every whim of the markets, consumer confidence and the overall national debt, then there's not much to trust in when things start looking bad. However, if you believe that you are experiencing certain things in life as a part of your learning journey, it makes it a lot easier to see the silver lining – or better yet – the opportunities that are available in a marketplace where there is fear.

You really need to see all things as they should be. If there is an economic downturn, then this means some reshuffling of people, new opportunities for growth, and a focus on or an appreciation for the more important things in life. If things were supposed to be different – they would have been. If the economy is on an upswing, then you get to explore more ways of creating abundance and appreciate all the great things you're seeing and creating in life. Again, if things were supposed to be different – it would have been.

Blindsided By God's Plan

There are only two ways to live your life. One is as though nothing is a miracle. The other is as though everything is a miracle.
– Albert Einstein

Superman grew up on a farm before he learned to fly. He learned important principles from his adopted parents on the farm. His parents always encouraged him and were amazed by his potential. Great parents see great potential and great leaders do the same. People who see greater potential in others and in themselves are superheroes in this world.

I found my farmer. His name was Jeff Allen. He was a business coach and life strategist who really did grow up as a farmer. Instead of studying successful people to see how he could imitate them, he came at success from the angle of, "How can everyone, no matter who they are, experience more intention, love and abundance in their life?" I met this plowboy from Idaho after I started working again for the technology company that I worked for before going to the e-Learning company. Jeff came in to do some training for the product management team I was on and he helped me clarify my dreams to create my own business by building a karate studio where I grew up. Jeff helped me align my self-talk, goals, and intentions, so that the Universe made magic happen. I left the corporate world, followed my dream, and the studio grew so fast it was almost overwhelming.

Like many stops along the way to success and fulfillment in life, when you run out of dream, the dream runs out of you. Building the karate studio was only part of my dream. I wanted to write and I was feeling stuck again, both in my business and in my personal life. I felt a strong impression to go back to the farmer and drink from his well of awareness and intention. When I called Jeff and mentioned my desire to get involved in a writing project, he laughed and said, "I was just meditating the other day and had a strong impression I needed to write down what I've learned over the past several years of coaching. And here you are Adam, right on time." We decided I should go through Jeff's personal ten-week, one-on-one Intentional Vision program to prepare for coauthoring a book.

I started to come down with a head cold the day I was supposed to start my first one-on-one coaching session with Jeff. It was a cold and overcast day in November. I remember taking a few aspirin before driving into Boise during the morning commute from my sister's house. My body ached and I wasn't thinking straight, but my mind was racing. I could have been in perfect health and it could have been a beautiful day for all I cared. I was excited to get started, both on my dream of writing a book and embarking on a new experience in life.

I had reviewed many of the leadership training chapters I received a few years earlier from Jeff. I also had the CD player going, listening to the same leadership chapters on my car stereo. I was doing everything I could to prepare myself for the one-on-one training journey I was about to jump into.

I arrived right on time and entered Jeff's office. He gave me a big embrace and said, "It's great to see you! How was the trip up?" I told him about how I was fighting off a cold and that it wasn't an easy trip to make late at night. I told him I'd pulled into my sister's place after midnight the night before and had a rough time sleeping during the night.

Jeff overrode my negative experience by saying, "I'm so glad you made it then, we're going to have a great time exploring who Adam really is!"

We sat down across the desk from each other and eased into the conversation. I fully thought we'd jump into the written material I'd been going through the last couple of days. Jeff, however, had no intention of starting there. He had other plans to open my mind to my own potential. Instead he asked, "Do you believe that this life is about making choices and having agency?"

Wow! That was a different way to start a coaching session. I wondered where this one question might take us. I had no problem with this direction in my beliefs, "Yes, I do believe this life has a lot to do with our choices."

He leaned forward a little, looked me straight in the eye and asked, "If this life experience is all about choice and agency, then do you believe you sat down with God before this experience and planned it out together?" That question rocked me backward a bit. I sat back in my chair and felt thunderstruck. The more I thought about it, the more profound it became, and the deeper I felt the answers swirling around in my mind like thunderstorms about to erupt.

What really got me was the idea that I had something to do with the planning of my entire life beforehand. Jeff repeated the question,

"If it's all about agency and choice, do you believe it's possible you planned your entire experience out with God?"

The enormity of the different thoughts I had to play out in my head was overwhelming. I sat there stunned, not by any fear of the idea, but of how true it felt! It was that aha! moment when God seems to be resonating within you. Each new idea that came to mind felt like it wasn't coming from my head, but my heart. My whole being vibrated and I felt like I was on fire, being consumed by the idea. It swept over me like a wave. The answer that came to mind with such force was, "Yes! If it is all about agency and choice, and I do believe in a loving God, then of course I sat down and planned this life experience with Him!"

I could envision the entire conversation with my Creator. I could see how each experience, both bad or good, failure or success, mistake or inspired act would play out to give me more experience and a better understanding of my Creator and of me as a kind of superhero. And believing that God was an all knowing being able to see the beginning to the end, I'm sure God could enlighten me enough to show me how my life would play out according to God and my plan. I believe if I had gone home that day, without learning anything else, my life would have changed completely.

The only source of knowledge is experience.
– Albert Einstein

My mind started to turn to the negative things in life and some of the challenging questions that constantly plague man's intelligence. So what is it we're supposed to do or learn in this short life experience? How is it that this life seems so long or maybe so short? Why are you facing these challenges or receiving so many opportunities? Why is there so much sickness, sadness, war, crime and despair in the world or just the opposite, why are there so many good people or so much beauty all around us? What about religion and its affect for good or bad in all of this experience?

Now you may believe in Buddha, Allah, or Christ or you may simply believe that there is some kind of Supreme Being or Central

Source running the show. Whatever your belief system and whatever name you give to your Creator, here are a few challenging questions that will change your perspective on this life. If you believe in a loving God and you believe you are one of God's children, wouldn't it make sense that you were the deciding factor on how you would live this life experience to get the greatest spiritual growth?

If you don't believe you had a choice in the matter, that your Creator simply put you here to test you, then take a closer look at this life experience. *All thinking is the process of making choices. It's agency on a life continuum. This whole human experience is directly related to choice. Choice is embedded in every act, every thought, every emotion, every belief, and every response you have to life's experiences. Your reality is based on your choices.*

Just for a minute, if you ask yourself the question of having had some prior choice about your life, how does it change the way you look at this life? It really boils down to one concept – *you own your life experience or you don't*. You are either a leader or you are a victim. You either see yourself as the author of your life – before, during and after or you are just here in chaos.

If you choose to believe you had a say in the matter, you'll start seeing that no matter what happens to you, you chose it – so then the question becomes, what can you learn from this experience now that you're living it? That's the right question to ask. Instead of asking yourself, "Why is this happening to me?" – which comes from an "I'm living in chaos mentality" – you'll start saying to yourself, "I own this experience, now what can I learn from this?" If you believe you chose the circumstances of your life, now you are empowered in making better choices about how you view and embrace this experience. After all, there is only one thing someone can't take away from you, your ability to choose your attitude.

Everything can be taken from man but one thing: the last of the human freedoms – to choose one's attitude in any given set of circumstances, to choose one's own way.
– Viktor E. Frankl, Psychiatrist and Nazi death camp survivor

Now I have to pause here to make sure you, the reader, realizes that the way Jeff approaches each coaching client is based on each person's identity profile and by listening to his own intuition. It's because of his style that he is so successful with his clients. Therefore, it makes it hard to reduce everything down into ink on a page for every personality. There are many principles and exercises in this book that will help everyone, because each person comes back with a different answer – an answer for himself or herself. That is the true beauty of this Intentional Vision process. It is open to the most important interpretation of all – yours.

I later asked Jeff how he goes through this same idea of identifying the core principles of this life with others. His answer is by making the connection between love, self-agency (your ability to choose), and freedom to create intentionally.

Jeff jumped to the white board and drew a circle and placed the word, "Love" in the middle of the circle. "Do you believe that love in all its forms, is what creates and is the power that holds the universe together in its ever expanding state?"

I smiled and said, "Yes, if love is a state of creation as you've told me before, then it is the driving and binding energy of the universe."

Jeff smiled as if he enjoyed seeing the enlightenment I'd gained. "Then can you have or experience love if you don't have self-agency and choice?" He drew a second circle and placed the phrase "Self-agency" in the center.

I thought about whether or not that was true. I couldn't refute it. Everything comes down to choice. Every creation is born out of choice. I shook my head, "I guess not."

"Can you experience true love, if you are not accountable for your choices?" Jeff asked.

I surmised that if you are not accountable for your choices, then you can't experience true love and enlightenment.

Jeff drew the last circle up on the board, wrote the word "Create" and turned back to me, "Can you experience freedom or the ability to create if you're not accountable or responsible for your choices?"

I wasn't sure about this one, so I simply repeated the question back to him rhetorically, "I don't know, can you experience freedom if you're not accountable for your choices?"

Jeff drew lines between the three circles, then looked over his shoulder at me. "Freedom is defined here as having more choices or the opportunity to exercise your choice to create or co-create with God. If you are not responsible for your choices, you will find you have fewer choices and less freedom to create. And for that matter, you will experience less love and abundance and more fear and scarcity in your life." Jeff drew another curved line back to love. "More freedom results in more love and abundance and that is how people start to understand the laws of Intentional Vision and why we are born with those primal emotions [love and be loved, experience self-agency and desire to create something] already programmed into our souls."

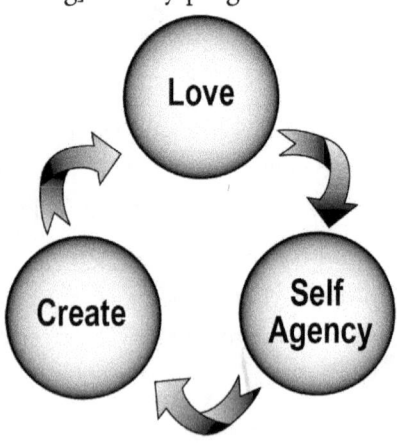

My Experience With The Conversation With God

After the realization that, "Yes, I could have planned this whole life experience out with God beforehand," settled into my head, the more I knew I owned this life experience. There wasn't anything that could come my way that I couldn't find a reason for it. The only problem is when do we realize the importance of the event as a learning tool – days, weeks or years afterwards or do we realize in the moment. If we do see the purpose in every event, when it's happening to us, we become an observer in our own life?

When we get stuck in life or when catastrophes happen to us, doesn't time seem to last forever? But how long is this lifetime, really? Is it as long as it seems, or is it nothing more than a simple experience in an eternal journey? Many people across the globe, regardless of their faith, believe that there is more than just this life experience. Wayne Dyer, a distinguished life motivator, says, *"If life is eternal, then this isn't life."*

So if a vast majority of people believe in some kind of eternity, then how long is this life? Time, as man has created it, is all based on motion. In our terms, we've taken the motion of the earth in one revolution and made it a day. Then we've taken the time to make one revolution around the sun and made that a year. Everything from a millisecond to a light year is based on the motions that we perceive here on earth.

More than a few ancient spiritual writings state that a thousand years to us, is one day to God. Just for the sake of it, let's take this variation of time of a thousand years being as a day to God and do some simple math:

24 hours	=	1,000 years
12 hours	=	500 years
6 hours	=	250 years
3 hours	=	125 years
1.5 hours	=	62.5 years

In fact, if you just want a factor to multiply by – one minute of God's time is equal to around 1.44 years of our time. You think time flies, well now you can really put it in perspective and understand why. If you live to be between 62 to 80 years old, you would be here in this life experience for about an hour and a half to two hours in God's time. What can you do in one and a half to two hours? You could take a short trip or a hike. You could go to a theatrical play or watch a movie or a TV program. You could have a good conversation with friends or with family. You could spend some time reading a book or researching a topic you enjoy. Face it, there's not much you can do in an hour and a half to two hours, is there?

But can an hour and a half to two hours make a difference in your life? In our life experience, a decision to change your direction in life takes but a moment. You can read a quote or witness an event that leaves a lasting impression. A new idea enlightens your mind in an instant. You can experience deep love or deep fear in a matter of seconds. You can change someone's attitude within a minute or two by smiling, telling a joke, or paying a compliment. A lot of growth can take place in a short amount of time, especially if you are focused on what's important.

> *I am convinced that He (God) does not play dice.*
> – Albert Einstein

Another way to look at life within the eternities is to try and conceive what eternity means, which is very difficult in our current life experience, because everything has a beginning and an end. I once heard a great example of what an eternity might be like. Imagine a sphere the size of the earth made of solid marble. Every 1,000 years a seagull flies up to the marble sphere and rubs its beak back and forth twice on the surface of the sphere and then flies away. When the marble sphere has completely eroded away from the seagull rubbing on it, that is an eternity.

It's hard to imagine how long it would take to wear away the earth-sized marble isn't it, especially if the thousand years we're talking about is in God's time and not ours. That would be approximately 131 million years in our time between each time the seagull came back to have a scratch! So for those of you who believe in a creator and evolution, and who believe that the earth is about four billion years old, that is a little less than 11,000 years for God. Going back to our eternal flock of seagulls and earth-sized marble sphere – that is not even 'scratching the surface' of time for an eternal being like God, and for us, is it?

Because this life experience is so short in the eternal perspective, of course we could have planned this life experience out! This belief alone of having planned out this life with God – and making choices about your experiences – brings about powerful changes. So I ask you, do *YOU own your life experience?* Do you believe you had any say in your experience and that you still have a say in your experience?

The thoughts about me planning this life experience with God resonated long after my coaching session with Jeff. It gives me more perspective on life. It helps me be more of an observer in my own experience, much like the ancient eastern philosophies that speak about a state of enlightenment. In a way, this concept both satisfies the people who believe that everything happens for a reason, because it is part of your destiny and it satisfies the thought that we are ultimately a significant part of our own progression in this life and in the eternities.

I've also shared this new insight with a few others, to whom I've felt the need to pass it to and I've watched as they've realized what this means. You really have to be ready to accept that everything happens for a reason – and you are the reason.

As I've shared this idea of planning this life experience out with our Creator, people often experience fear and make statements like, "Well if that were the case, then what would be the point of doing anything, if it's all about fate?" In this case, they are simply expressing their fear that they don't have any choice or agency now that they're in this experience. Nothing could be farther from the principle of self-agency. Why would you design a house and not build it? Why would you write a movie, play or book and not make it or publish it? Why would you form a business plan and not build the business? If you create anything in any way in your mind, don't you want to experience it? Your mind is always looking for better ways to experience this life. In fact, daydreaming is simply your mind finding new ways to create happiness in your life.

Once you have the blueprints to your house and start building it, don't you still have many choices to make? Don't you still have creative license with the end result? You may change a wall here or there. You may change your mind on the color scheme. You go to different stores and select the cabinets, the flooring, the window coverings and everything else in your new home. Then when it's time to move in, don't you often buy a few new pieces of furniture that will enhance the look and feel of your new home? The same could be said with any plan that turns into a physical creation, whether it's a movie script or an invention or a plan for your new business venture. You have choices and self-agency all the way through the process.

The point of giving you this idea of planning your life experience beforehand is that you now have the ability and awareness to own everything in your life – the wins, the losses, the love and the fear, the roses and the thorns and the things that even seem out of your immediate control. You are now the 'Soul Proprietor' of your life. If God and the natural flow of the universe is about love and love motivation, then you can't be forced to do anything and still feel love. The only way to measure love is to be willing to let it go and if it loves you, it will return to you. With that being the case, you would have had to choose everything in your life – where you were born, who your family is and what belief system you embrace or don't embrace.

It also makes sense that if you chose this experience, you would choose your own weakness to overcome so you can learn, grow and experience your greatest triumphs. In other words, you chose, at some level, your kryptonite. Now how do you choose to use it?

If you want personal growth, if you want a feeling of freedom, no matter what happens to you or around you, then own your life! Be your own Soul Proprietor and superhero and you will have the greatest joy possible. So you need to ask yourself, "Did I plan this whole life experience with God or my Creator?" Let that idea resonate and see where it takes you.

Making It Crystal Clear

1) In order to succeed you need to trust life and that you have a purpose in life.

2) Believe you have great potential and that potential was meant to be – planned out.

3) See beyond this existence and know that you learn through your mistakes.

4) Own this life experience – every triumph and every failure as well as events you can't control.

Intentional Vision Exercises

1) Write boldly on something you can look at while looking at your eyes in a mirror, "I LOVE MYSELF AND I PLAY TO WIN!" or "I TRUST GOD AND THE UNIVERSE AND I PLAY TO WIN!" (Feel free to change this statement to fit your beliefs in a higher power or source.) Say this 100 times per day. Be sure you go to the place in your heart that causes you to feel trust; you are on purpose with positive self-talk. Again, if you really want the change, look deeply into your eyes – into your soul – and say it from the heart. It will feel strange at first, but soon you'll get it.

2) Make three lists:
   - Write a list of the things you've criticized about yourself and others today.

- A list of things that disappointed you.
- A list of things you failed at.
    - Each day, write a new list and you'll find that some items remain on the list every day, but commonly by the end of the week you'll have a very short list.
    - Each day after completing your three lists, throw your lists in the trash and say to yourself – "I'm letting go. I'm so done holding onto these negative, toxic emotions!"

3) Now write in your journal a list of activities, relationships, things, or feelings that make you happy or feel in abundance – you will keep building this list as you go through each chapter or each week of the Intentional Vision process.

4) Activities: Start looking for a method to nurture your emotional hygiene. Your Innate mind is the core of who you are. Find activities that are nurturing and rewarding to your Innate mind. These activities will create calmness in your mind, which will help you develop a much greater trust in the Universe.

5) Continue to write in a journal the wins you experienced this week.

Chapter 4

Trust Your Powers In The Universe And Discover Your Kryptonite

The following is a poem written long ago by Dale Wimbrow and modified through the years to create a different reflection on ourselves:

The Guy In The Glass

> When you get what you want in your struggle for self
> And the world makes you king for a day
> Just go to the mirror and look at yourself
> And see what that man has to say.
>
> For it isn't your father or mother or wife
> Whose judgment upon you must pass
> The fellow whose verdict counts most in your life
> Is the one staring back from the glass.

You can fool the whole world down the highways of life
And get pats on your back as you pass
But the final reward will be heartaches and tears
If you've cheated the man in the glass.

Others may think you add up to a sum
And they call you a wonderful guy
But if the man in the glass says you're only a bum
As you look him straight in the eye.

It is up to you to change the you
So take a good look inside
To do this with love is the ultimate clue
For if not you will find him defied.

He's the fellow to please, never mind the rest
For he's with you clear to the end
And you've passed your most dangerous, difficult test
If the man in the glass is your friend.

The Second Law of Intentional Vision – Trust Your Powers In The Universe And Discover Your Kryptonite
(Week 3 Reading Assignment)

The first Law of Intentional Vision is trusting that the Universe has everything you need to find absolute freedom, love and happiness. The Second Law of Intentional Vision that will help you build freedom and love is to Trust Yourself In the Universe.

This may seem like a simple concept, but I challenge you to go up to every person you know and ask them to advise you on something you can do that will enhance your life (and make it a big something).

The thoughts of asking someone for advice may cause you feelings of insecurity; fear might start to creep in. But I have to remind you that "if it is going to be, it is up to me (you)." When a good idea or solution to an obstacle is revealed, act on the advice NOW. Don't wait!

It is important to take immediate action because if you don't your brain will accept failure as the safer method and your 'lack of confidence' patterns will be reinforced.

Most people will not ask for help or guidance because they simply don't trust themselves enough. There is a fear that if they take a piece of advice and fail, they will feel ashamed and feel like a failure. But if you trust yourself, any negative outcomes will be seen as setbacks that might seem as a detour from your personal freedom; but in reality this is only a learning tool. Remember that mistakes are your friends and are truly the only way to learn. When you see a setback as a learning experience, you are on your way to trusting yourself and getting the freedom you deserve.

When you trust the Universe is in a total abundance of opportunities, and that there is far more than anyone could ever acquire, then it is time to trust yourself. The individuals that trust themselves and see what it is they want take action immediately.

Let me explain more on the bread example from the last chapter. OK, you need a loaf of bread. And you know a store down the street that always has one, so you set out to get the loaf of bread. As you back out of the driveway, a speeding car almost hits you. Do you give up because you don't trust yourself enough to keep going? Of course not!

Next, as you are driving down the street you get a flat tire; do you give up and go home? Heck no! Will you eventually solve the car problem and get to the store? Yes!

You might get to the store a lot later than you thought but you will eventually get to the store, because you want the bread. Then while you are walking down the store aisle toward the bakery section, you see a sign that says "Sorry, out of bread".

Now, you might want to blame the Universe that the bread wasn't there, but if you believe that there is another place that has bread and if you trust your ability to go get it, you will immediately take action and go to the next store.

Your decision will happen so quickly you did not even feel you made a decision. You just acted. Everything in life, and I mean everything, is just the same. If you want that perfect something, but don't believe that it is out there, then you are not even going to put any effort toward obtaining it.

Also, if you don't trust yourself, you will live in a scarcity thinking lifestyle. If you don't trust yourself, scarcity will control your life and you will be afraid to do almost anything. You will hoard your possessions, such as having a closet full of clothes that don't fit anymore or are so outdated you never wear them anyway.

But let's say you believe that the perfect something is waiting for you. When you trust yourself, you will take immediate action to go get it. You will get started so quickly that it will seem like a decision was not even made. You will find out where to go and not have any consideration about what to say when you get there, or how to say it. You will simply be living a life of abundance – one that is waiting for you. Do you know what will happen when you get started? I've seen it time and time again… you will find someone that knows someone that might even know someone else; and to others it might seem like magic that you have such a perfect life. But in reality you simply trusted the Universe had that special thing waiting and you knew you had the ability to go make it happen.

If you trust the Universe has the kind of freedom you want, the next step is to trust your ability to go find it. Life is just like finding the loaf of bread. You might have a plan laid out to go to the store and get the bread, but if it is not there it's up to you to decide if you are going to keep looking.

The Universe has anything you want, more money, more happiness, more freedom, more _____ (fill in the blank). Now it is up to you to have enough trust in yourself to start looking for it, and to simply keep looking until you find it. The Universe is in total abundance, it is up to you to accept the abundance it offers.

Trusting yourself takes self-forgiveness and devotion to stay in tune with your desires. It is common that when the going gets tough the people in your life and the voices in your head will tell you to quit trying, to simply give up. Giving up can be a common theme for many and those that think this way are looking for a safer and easier method to accept failure. But the real failure is not trusting ourselves, thinking that you don't have the ability to get to know the real person inside, the one that can be trusted.

I mean really get to know who you are from a completely raw position, a position that is un-edited and uncooked, and a position that really is working by a standard of truths that are yours to trust. A person who really knows himself or herself has values and ideals that they know and live by. They have a trust in self by using their own visions as a guide and holding true to a Win – Win adult attitude.

But if you give up, it is because you did not trust yourself enough to keep going. You have not taken the time to get to know the real you inside. You are unable to let go of the past and stop judging yourself. I will positively guarantee that anyone who has achieved personal freedom did not do so in their first try. They had many attempts, many mistakes, and many disappointments. The richest or the happiest people tripped, fell down, and then got back up to find a way to get what they were looking for.

But ultimately they found that happiness comes from within, it comes from who we are and not what we do. They learned that who they are is far more important than what they do. If what you are doing is getting in the way of who you are, then you are living by someone else's dreams.

I am not suggesting that throwing in the towel is the solution to anything; I am suggesting that there are no accidents and that you are there for a reason. The people in your life right now are the ones that will help you advance into your next level of trust. It is up to you to teach those around you how to live a life that is sharing dreams, your dreams. By helping them win they will also be helping you win. It is important that you implement win-win in all the relationships in your life.

One of the key components of trusting yourself is self-judgment, because if you are in judgment you cannot experience justice. Self-judgment is a beginning point of self-defeat. When you are judging yourself it will create a despair that comes from within and it will deny your natural knowing of what your purpose is.

I also guarantee that people who have created wealth, and maintained it, were able to overcome negative self-judgment and trust that the Universe had what they wanted. They might have started their journey with some doubts about their ability, knowledge, or talents but found when they trusted themselves and started using their God-given talents, they become true to self. The beauty of self trust is that it attracts followers because the only way to lead others is by leading yourself first.

Those that have a well-defined self-trust are the ones that know their soul's purpose, they know and trust they have a meaning, a purpose in life. They have well-defined goals that keep them on purpose. I will make a pledge to you, that you too will have a well defined purpose in life by learning and living with a self trust, your ability to live on purpose and not off purpose will be well programmed in your life. Those who have a well-defined purpose and live with self-trust have an inner knowing of truth and a deep feeling of integrity with self.

You must trust your true potential, the one that gives you the passion for achievement. Your potential is a divine inner desire to achieve greatness and you are the only one that can stop you. Only you can determine that you do not have what it takes to achieve freedom or happiness. Only you can determine what you will do next to accomplish you life's purpose.

It does take a commitment to have faith, or raw intention, that you can accomplish your ultimate goal of freedom. It takes a self-image that overrides any negative thoughts or attitudes. Our subconscious is running programs that will hold a vision of who we should be, but our real goal is to let go and let God–to feel the joy of being who we are innately. Your innate is the most important, the one that requires nurturing, and the one that feels the love, the love you deserve to have at all times.

Now I know that you might have problems from the past, and challenges might hinder you from time to time throughout the process. But if you let go, and trust yourself, you will not give up. You must understand that through the process of choosing your thoughts, you in fact choose who you have become. And sometimes others make a choice for you, but then you did choose to allow others to make that choice.

Remember that if you don't choose, others will choose for you! Those that don't choose will allow sabotage programs to control their life; they allow the negative thoughts to become their outcome. And the things they fear the most are experienced in their future. It is really up to you to change your life and start living a life that you envision. You must start with the real you – are you funny, kind, do you enjoy life? Now I don't mean fake it till you make it, I mean a real down-to-earth feeling of knowing who you are, and being able to see yourself the way you want to be seen by others.

So let go, and I mean let go. Pay attention to the feeling of fear… and let go. Fear is the absence of love, so just let go of that fear and trust the Universe and trust yourself. This is an inside-out process, one that requires an absence of being a victim and requires you to be accountable for your success.

If someone is going to be successful then it might as well be you, and if not you, then who? And if that who is not you, then you chose it.

So…do your homework!

There is no level of trust I can give you that will overcome your inability to trust yourself and if you don't trust yourself others will fall out of trust with you.

By trusting that the Universe will provide for you…because it will, I can promise that when you trust yourself, you will not give up on the ultimate quest for whatever it is you want.

The Coach's Kryptonite

Before challenging me to look for my major weakness, Jeff related the following story from his youth: "I didn't understand my major weakness until I became a trainer. That's when my enlightenment came, when I started to ask myself, 'What is my major weakness?' In fact, I wasn't teaching about it until I went through a training session and the instructor said, 'You have to know what your major weakness is before you know what your purpose is.' And then all of it connected for me."

"When I was an infant, I had a bone marrow problem because of radiation fallout when they were popping off those nukes in Nevada. I ended up in the hospital and they thought I was going to die, but it obviously didn't happen."

I asked Jeff, "Where did you live?"

"I lived in eastern Idaho. That's what killed my dad and it killed a lot of people in Idaho. They have documents that say that they chose when to pop off those nukes based on the weather. They would do it when the wind was blowing toward non-populated, low importance areas, instead of when it was blowing toward places like Los Angeles or other parts of California."

"So that happened when I was a child and my mom was going through a lot of emotional struggles during the time while I was an infant. The point is that I was left at a lot of people's homes between mom's emotional challenges and my being sick. Life was going on and I was left to the side. My dad died when I was about two and a half years old. My mom remarried and right after she remarried, she had more emotional episodes. She was checking in and out of life, dealing with all the changes over the past few years. During that first five or six years of my life, I would leave the house and not come back until it was dark. That was the only reason I came home, because it was dark. I was very independent, and very isolated."

"From my parent's perspective, I was probably so hard to deal with that it was easier just leaving me alone. But we were living in the country and it didn't seem to matter. When I was six, seven or eight, I don't really know how old I was, here we are the country folk or if you want to think of it as the 'country mice.' And if you can imagine the 'city mouse' picture, my aunt, my mom's sister, Grace, drives up in a brand new yellow car with big fins on the back end. She has this pink scarf on and new shoes and she was 'dressed to the nines.' And mom has this mint plaid men's shirt on with holey jeans and worn out tennis shoes. Grace said to my mom, 'Glenna, let's go to town all day today, it'll be my treat.' She didn't call ahead, she just showed up. And of course my mother loved it, she practically hit the ceiling she was so excited.

I asked my mom, 'Can I go, can I go?' I followed her into the bedroom continually asking her, 'Can I go, can I go?' I follow her outside, still asking her the same thing. We got outside close to the driveway and my aunt Grace says, 'Oh come on Glenna, it will be a lot of fun. Let Jeff come.' So mom said, 'All right, go get your shoes on.' I ran in the house to get my shoes on."

Jeff slumped back in his seat as if all the air had been let out of him, "I don't know if it took me five minutes or five days, but when I came out of the house, they had left. I remember laying on the grass and crying, 'They left me again! They don't love me!' I was crying and sobbing and my heart was throbbing and I was experiencing all this pain."

"Well, after that experience, I went through life making sure that no one would leave me again. And if they were going to leave me, I was going to be the bully and chase them away, so that I knew why they were leaving. So when I go through all my negative experiences while I was growing up, that's the emotion that actually created them."

"Now the interesting thing about the emotion is that I believed the emotion and I only paid attention to the things that validated the emotion. I didn't pay attention to anything else. And the way that I can validate that is because when I went through high school, I do not remember my mother being at any athletic events or anything where I was receiving an award. I didn't believe that people who loved me would show up, wouldn't be there, or wouldn't take me with them. Then when I was an adult, I asked my brother, 'Did mom ever hang around you at events when we were growing up?' My brother said, 'She was there all the time. It pestered the heck out of me! It bugged me that she showed up at everything! I didn't want her there, but she was always there.' And yet, my experience was that she was never there."

"I just validated all my story saying that this is why I felt that way, but in reality that's the way I remembered the story. That's not the way the story could have been remembered. It could have been remembered in a lot of ways."

I asked Jeff, "So you're saying that she was there, you just didn't see her being there?"

He said, "It could have been, it very well could have been. I could have been hauled off to a relative's house one time in a whole year, and it seemed to me that I was there all the time, that I was never home, because I was at someone else's house. You see that is my memory. My memory tells me that I spent more time outside of the house and not in the house for the first five or six years of my life."

I wanted to make sure that I understood, so I asked, "There was an event and there was so much emotion attached to that event that it influences our habits?"

"Yes, we all have a major weakness. So even today, that will click for me and I'll get the thought of, 'I wonder if they're going to leave me, because they don't like me?' I still have that click in my mind that they don't like me and they are going to leave me. I have that emotion surface all the time. I haven't reprogrammed it, because it's really deeply seated. However, I am aware of it, so that when it does go off, I can remind myself, this is why I'm feeling this way, this is why that experience and emotions are showing up this way. All of us have a major weakness and almost all of our bad habits or self-destructive programs are attached to that one thing."

Jeff said, "Your assignment for this next week is to find out what your major weakness is. And when you know what your major weakness is, and can understand it, then you will be able to manage your attitudes, because your bad habits stem from your imprinted mind and they kick in to try and control the environment, so your innate self doesn't get hurt again."

Jeff also gave me the assignment to try out an attitude lift with my students or my leadership team at my karate studio. He said, "Pair your students off with other students about their same size and have partner A think really heavy thoughts and pretend like their feet are hooked to the floor. Then have partner B put their arms around them and lift them off the ground. Now partner A, don't let them lift you! You're thinking heavy thoughts. The majority of the students won't be able to lift their partner. It's amazing how that works. If you have someone who is really intentional, you will have a really hard time lifting them up. Think about going outside and lifting a bag of cement that weighs 180 pounds. You will realize that it is really heavy, that's really a lot of weight to lift. If the human body goes into that emotion that, 'I'm really heavy,' they will be very heavy."

"Now consider yourself to be very light, and it's easy to be lifted. And the other person will find that it's easy to lift them up. And the point of this exercise is that it's all about attitude that changes the experience. A person can't change their weight on the bathroom scales with attitude, but they can change the experience of how the weight is perceived.

You know, if you go into a room and think it's light, people start joking and laughing and having a good time. If you go in thinking that it's heavy and think heavy thoughts, you'll experience it that way."

I jumped in and said, "Are you doing the What-You-See-Is-What-You-Get thing to me again?"

Jeff laughed, smiled at me and said, "Well, I get to go eat lunch now."

Finding Kryptonite With Thai Food

I walked out of Jeff's office wondering, "What are my bad habits and what event or events might have triggered them?" It hit me right away. I made a conscious effort to watch the traffic as I crossed a very busy four-lane street. I knew I better be alert because my first inclination was to block out everything else as I thought about my new awareness about my major weakness. I wrote the following in my personal journal:

> My Major Weakness Is...
> December 17,
> I didn't have to go much farther than the sidewalk to realize what it was. Then I asked myself some qualifying questions to see if I had indeed found my weakness. Sure enough, I knew my weakness and immediately I thought about all my bad habits or things that I don't do well. They all stem from my not wanting to be committed! That's it in a nutshell – commitment to others! Now I just needed to find out why I felt that way. Was it some kind of betrayal I felt or now that I think about it, maybe it was some kind of failure that I experienced and I don't want to feel that kind of rejection or shame for failing.
> I had a great little lunch with my sister. I'm not sure if I've ever done a one-on-one lunch with just one sister. We talked about what I was going through in my training.
> I mentioned to my sister what Jeff had told me about searching for my weakness. I told her that I thought my weakness was commitment. Then I said something about that I might have felt betrayed some time earlier in my life. Instantly she came up with several examples of where I had been betrayed. However, they were examples from my high school days and I was looking for an event from my early childhood. Yet, I thought it was interesting that I seemed to have drawn some betrayal into my life. My sister mentioned having my friend from my senior year betray me and run off with my girl friend. My sister also brought up a girl I dated and to whom I almost proposed. She hooked up with someone else from work over a Christmas holiday

and I certainly did feel betrayed.

We also dug a little deeper into my sister's feelings and she came out with guilt being her main weakness. That was a keen insight, especially when she talked about all the different things she's done out of guilt. By the way, I had the Panang Curry and it was oh so good!

I went back to the office and told Jeff, "I know what my weakness is."

He said, "That was fast. I take it that your lunch with your sister was a good one to help you stay on your purpose?"

"Yes, it most definitely was." I was feeling a lot different than I did earlier with that feeling of being in synch with my own feelings and with being on purpose with people around me.

After relating my conversation to Jeff, I still felt at a loss, because I couldn't pinpoint, like he could, the event that exposed my major weakness. In fact in the subsequent few years since the first awareness of my major weakness, I've often felt jealous of those people who could identify the event that exposed their major weakness. That is no longer the case. While going through this process again in order to become a greater life coach, I finally figured out where my need to hide from fear–or where fear of commitment–came from.

I went through the process of going even deeper and asking, "What emotion is under that?" What I found was in helping someone find their major weakness; I discovered an even deeper level to mine.

One of my first traumatic memories was that of hiding under a table in the kitchen. My mother was at the kitchen sink sobbing terribly. Our neighbor and landlord had her arm around my mother consoling her. I didn't know much at the time, because I was only about four years old, but I did know that something terrible had happened. My grandmother had passed away. I wouldn't find out until I was a teenager that she had committed suicide.

Like I said, I've been trying to figure out what the event was that had caused a breach in trust in life and exposed enough pain to reinforce the pattern of protection in my brain. Just recently, at a neighbor's funeral, I brought up that early memory with our former neighbor and landlord. She gave me more insight into that terrible event, so I could take a closer look at how it had impacted my mother and me.

My neighbor said, "Your mom was very busy with you little kids. She had you and your sister and she had a newborn baby, too. Your grandmother had called a few times asking your mom to come down because she was feeling depressed. This wasn't an uncommon occurrence. Your grandmother often called your mother, hoping to get some kind of help getting out of her depression. Your mom and I had just finished painting part of the house a light lavender when the call came about your grandmother. It wasn't too long after that call that your mom and I had to repaint that part of the house a different color, because she couldn't stand the color lavender. Now I know I didn't pick out the lavender color. It was your mother who originally picked the color, but she couldn't stand it after your grandmother died."

It was then that I realized that as a young boy I had picked up on more than just the pain of my grandmother dying. I had also picked up on my mother's self-anger and anguish for not being there for her mother in her time of need. For years my mother hated the color purple and lavender. It's only as she's grown older that she's begun to tolerate and let that color back into her life.

My emotion while I was under the table was that of hiding from the fear I was experiencing and feeling like in some way I had caused the pain. I felt the judgment and the rejection all within my own mind and I felt the pain my mother was going through. I don't want to be judged and rejected and my way of not committing fully in my relationships, in my activities and my business is that any time fear comes up, I want to go hide under the table – not literally – but figuratively and in my actions. When I'm in scarcity, I'm under the table, under the blanket, under the radar, living under cover. I'm not living with any boldness in my life. When I'm not in fear, I'm dancing on the table, jumping on the bed, saying here I am, and living boldly, not caring whether or not I'm accepted, because I accept myself.

When I initially told Jeff I didn't know where the experience of not committing came from, he said, "It's not the view that you need to know where it started. It's just to acknowledge it. Now you've got your brain cells firing on it."

"Yeah, they're firing all over the place," I said.

"Now you're creating this new level of awareness to put the thought out there to say, 'Now every time sabotage comes up in your world, you can point at this emotion that caused it. It will come at the time of crisis or it causes the crisis, one or the other. We could say that it almost has an entity, identity or humor all of its own. And it stirs your course to get you there again, so you can validate yourself.

I jokingly said, 'Oh! Sure enough...there's that commitment bug!"

Jeff added, "Yeah, sure enough, I'm normal, there's my major weakness talking to me again."

Owning Your Major Weakness

Here are a few ways to discover your major weakness. First, look back over your life and find all the events that bring up pain for you, including deaths, divorces or breakups, catastrophes, really bad days, crimes committed against you, or whatever else comes to mind and find a common thread that runs through them. If you approach this with curiosity and with the thought of "What is life's mirror trying to teach me about myself?" you'll start seeing your life in a new way; in a clearer way.

Another way to find your major weakness is look back on your early childhood, probably before the age of eight, and find the experiences that were the most traumatic for you. Then ask yourself, "How am I protecting myself from similar pain?" You'll find that the same way you protect yourself will come up again and again in your experience. Because this protection doesn't serve your purpose any longer, it now manifests as your bad habits. It might not be a single traumatic event at all; instead it might be a series of closely related events that helped forge your imprinted mind to a protective mode.

Just like mistakes are your friends for improvement, knowing and owning your major weakness is a significant step toward trusting yourself. It's much easier to look at any mistake you make or problem that comes up and see if it is linked to your major weakness. If you own it, then you will learn from it and in that way your major weakness is your best friend in helping you learn what you need to in order to experience love and success.

Jeff spoke about another client he had that wouldn't accept that he was attracting his negative experiences through his major weakness. Jeff said, "I had a client who I consistently wouldn't show up for. And he was a really Green personality and it was very tough on him. I finally had to say to him, "I don't know why you're calling out for this? I don't know why you need to prove to yourself that people don't show up in your life? I asked him, 'Who in your life ever shows up for you?'

He said, 'Nobody.'

I said, 'I see why!'"

I filled in the part, "because he was always putting that emotion out there."

Jeff continued, "Yeah, I said, 'I've never had a problem showing up for anybody like I haven't shown up for you.' Now he really had a hard time shifting that emotion, because he kept wanting to make it about him and he wouldn't own and honor the experience. Because if he chose to own and honor it, everyone would have shown up in his life, but he wasn't willing to do that, especially his wife, that's the saddest thing. His poor wife is on antidepressants, she's totally checked out of life, so for him no one is showing up in his life. That's really why he took the course and he didn't even know it. And when I exposed it to him, he didn't get it, he didn't want to choose to get it."

"He didn't buy into it then?" I asked.

Jeff replied, "I've only had a few individuals that don't get it. And it's because he didn't do the homework. If you do the homework and you're diligent about it, you will get it and you will own it. Everyone who does the homework gets it."

I thought this was very interesting since Jeff always puts at the end of each homework assignment. "I have to stress to you again that it is so important to do your homework: It is the way you show commitment to yourself."

There was that commitment word again. However, I felt good that I have always been committed to doing this Intentional Vision process. If you're not willing to invest the time, the money and the emotion in yourself, you just won't get the rewards of a deeper self-awareness and a personal intimacy. It's the fair exchange with the Universe and with yourself. I guess if you show the emotion–show the effort–you'll be shown the love.

As you begin to see that all the major catastrophes, injuries, pain, broken relationships, deaths, and anything else that caused you pain was there to teach you something – don't just say, "Life sucks!" or "Life is unfair!" Dig deeper to see if it's about your relationship with people, if you don't commit, if it's about learning to trust God, yourself or others, if it's about holding on to certain experiences or rules that don't serve you, like the need to see life as being fair for everyone. If you own your life, you'll see that everyone's life is fair, because they chose it that way. Look and you will find what your major weakness is.

If you look even deeper into all of your bad habits, like procrastination, pushing people away, overspending too often, excessive eating, staying up too late, being a workaholic, over processing everything, or anything else that holds you back, it is all related back to that fear from which you're subconsciously trying to keep yourself safe.

The greatest part of taking on your life and finding your major weakness is that you will be aware of your weakness whenever it comes up. You can smile and joke about it. You might even want to give it a name or a label, so you know and can easily move it aside in your mind and move toward your purpose. Regardless of what you want to do with your major weakness, you can make it your strength.

Freedom and Forgiveness

One way to know if you trust yourself is if you are willing to forgive yourself or allow yourself to make mistakes. If you can't allow mistakes in your life without beating yourself up, you don't trust yourself. How do you get away from this behavior? The strange thing is you have to ask yourself what your mistake is teaching you about you. Now a lot of people will immediately say, "I'm an idiot" or "I must be stupid!" Okay, so what do you learn from saying those things about yourself? Yeah, you've got it – you don't trust and love yourself. So we're back to where we started – what is your mistake or weakness teaching you? Take a deeper look – maybe while looking in the mirror and affirming yourself.

Once you figure out what your mistake is teaching you and you still haven't let go of the feeling of guilt or self-anger or unhappiness, then you have to ask yourself, "Is this mistake trying to help me learn something else?" Listen to your thoughts and feelings as you ask this last question. If the answer comes back that there isn't anything else to learn, simply say to yourself (in the mirror or aloud) I forgive myself of the negative learning and I choose to experience learning and peace. Then let it go.

You may wonder when are you forgiven? The answer is when you've learned the lesson the mistake was teaching you and you choose to let go. It can be instantaneous. If you carry the mistake around with you, you are either saying that you want that mistake because it gives you an excuse to fail or that you don't love and trust yourself. If you know your major weakness, you'll know pretty quickly why you've chosen to carry your mistake.

By the way, the introvert personalities (Blue, Teal and Green) seem to carry their pain longer and do not want to give up the burden of their mistakes. However, when these people learn how to forgive themselves, life gets so much easier and they don't often get stuck or carry the weight of the past around.

Mistakes Are My Friends

> *The man who makes everything that leads to happiness depends upon himself, and not upon other men; [this man] has adopted the very best plan for living happily.*
> –Plato

Jeff asked the question, "What do you think it takes to be a great leader?"

"Lots of things I suppose and it depends on the situation we're put in," I said.

"That's true and it's our perspective about taking charge of our life or being a leader in our life, which hearkens back to the way we were trained as a child. The psychology of life leadership is very similar to how a baby learns to walk." Jeff held his hand above the desk as if he were following something moving across the desk. "The baby is crawling along and figuring out this crawling experience and pretty soon the baby experiences a standing experience. Somewhere between the standing experience and curiosity the baby doesn't think about going somewhere, the baby just starts walking." Jeff motioned with his hand as mimicking a miniature baby walking across the desktop. His walking fingers stop for a moment, then Jeff said, "When the baby is seen in that walking state, everyone claps and smiles. If the baby recognizes that someone is watching him, the baby falls down almost in that very instant." Jeff's hand flopped on the desk. "And in all this excitement, we know that the baby is going to fall down."

Jeff drew back his hands to his lap and interlocked them across his stomach. With a little shrug, he said, "Now the goal is to walk. The opposite of walking would be crawling or falling, right? If every time our child fell down we spanked or yelled at him or her, you can see that very quickly the child wouldn't want to learn to walk. The child would soon associate walking with failure and pain and decide that crawling was the best way to move and still win."

As I look back on this conversation I can see how the parents simply trust that their child will work things out and learn in due time how to walk. We have to understand that God is doing the same with us. It's like he's allowed us to play on a playground knowing full well that we might get hurt or pushed around or feel scared. It's something we get to learn and experience, so he trusts that we will learn what we need to learn in life in due time.

Getting back to what Jeff was saying in our first session and how we tend to not hold ourselves in trust and love he said, "We understand that the learning to walk experience is important. Yet, we have raised ourselves in that fear and failure mentality. Whenever we challenge ourselves to do something new and exciting, and then we fall down, how do we react? We spank ourselves and tell ourselves that we are bad or wrong or that we can't do it. 'I'm a bad person because I didn't lose the weight or get the job or accomplish my goals.'"

Jeff pointed to his head and said, "The challenge is that we've raised ourselves with this fear-based program and it's in there running all the time." Jeff raised his voice a little and in a very matronly way said, "'If you try that and you fail or fall down, someone's going to spank you.' Isn't that the way we feel sometimes?" I nodded my head, knowing that I often feel and think this way. I know I beat myself up the more I don't measure up to some artificial version I've created for myself.

Jeff said, "The concept of making mistakes and how the program is running in our heads is important, so we can take on that next purposeful experience in our lives." Jeff stood up and then acted like he was going to fall, then stood up straight again. "The individual who says it's easier to fall down than to get up, that's the Victim. They have the ability to create a story in their head that it's safer to crawl than to walk, so I'm going to crawl through my life. And the opposite of a Victim is a leader or a Co-Creator. The leader or Co-Creative person can say, 'You know I fell down, but I'm going to get back up.' The falling down and getting back up is nearly 100% reliant upon the individual's self-trust or self-love. If that energy, passion, or love isn't in our body, then it will feel safer to stay down."

It struck me that Co-Creators learn to walk and then run, while Victims continue to crawl through life. You get to choose which way you want to experience life. However, unlike the instance of a toddler learning to walk, the only one who is most likely going to beat you up for falling down is you.

I remember talking to my friend, who had served in an ecclesiastical position at a county jail. I asked him about the different people he met at the jail and whether or not they felt like they were guilty. His reply was, "Almost every one of the inmates says that they're innocent. And what's amazing is that they're convinced that they are all innocent. It's not one or two of them that think this either, it's almost every one of them." I wondered about the psychology behind this, are they all in denial of why they're really behind bars? You can't get much more stuck in life than being in jail. How is it that someone, who has committed a crime, can think of himself or herself as innocent? I'm sure there a few rare cases, but I believe they don't want to accept their life or who they are, or how they got to a place where they are locked away from the rest of society. In other words, they don't own their experience and they deny their mistakes are learning tools.

Faith and Weakness

I've realized that commitment to others is also about faith and intention in people. If I'm not committed, then I can't be bold in my life. At least that's the case with me. I can commit or be bold with myself, and I often do. I will spend money on my own education. I will create good habits of reading positive books and listen to motivational information. However, when it comes to committing to others, that's where I've lacked in the past.

I've been taught all my life about faith – that it is knowing without seeing and that it is like a seed, if you plant it and nourish it, the seed will grow. I've experienced faith and with it a few miracles. What I didn't realize is that faith is not reserved for the saintly, nor is it only for the religious. Faith and intention is for everyone in every aspect of life. It is what helps the gardener or the farmer to plant their crop and help it grow. Faith and intention is for the businessman or businesswoman who puts their heart into creating a business plan and then continuously following the plan and persuading others in his or her effort. Faith and intention is for the mother and the father, who nurture and believe in their children and see more in their children than they can possibly see in themselves. Faith and intention is for the athlete who continues to push their body to new levels of endurance or skill or for the team who faces a challenge without fear. Faith is plain and simply trust.

I now have greater faith and trust in myself and I get to review how that can apply to commitment to others. I get to be more bold and courageous with others. My first reaction to realizing my major weakness was to spot where I was not committed to my karate students and to their development. I also found myself feeling that I was letting a few of them off too easily. I had a few parents who came to me for one reason or the other to see if they could be released from their karate agreements. I found that I had a lot more passion to see them both stay in the program, so they could grow, but also to be more committed to themselves.

I remembered when Jeff told me that he is mostly driven by a passion that borders on anger. I thought that was strange, since he's a coach and the first question he asks you is, "Will you allow me to love you?" If that's how he starts every coaching relationship, how is it that he can be driven by anger? Jeff told me, "There is such a thing as righteous anger. It just makes me mad when people don't get it. When they choose not to get it!" When Jeff says, "to get it," he means to understand, become more aware of their purpose and own their lives. In other words, he is committed, and therefore that's why he gets angry when other people aren't committed to making a positive change in their lives.

Jeff made it clear to me that righteous anger is not about throwing a temper tantrum, it is more about seeing what the person can become or do and understanding that their current choices will not get them there. Righteous anger is passion and love with a little fire under it. It's about looking deep inside yourself to see that you are doing all you can to help the other person and still allowing them to experience their lessons in life.

This type of anger or passion is not about fear, it is about love and the ability to create something more. Jeff said, "I guess this type of anger, if you want to call it that, is a high level of energy that is directed in a purposeful way. It's the way I experience being really raw with people. To other people I may seem calm, direct and strong with my comments, but on the inside there is that fire, that passion that drives me to help other people. Yet, I know that in order to honor love motivation, I always have to honor their experience and know that they are gaining their lessons from their choices in life. The anger or passion or whatever that high level of energy is keeps me 'raw' with people, so they understand what it is to own and honor their experience."

Jeff gets that passionate anger when he sees a person make a choice or a conscious break of trust in a person's life, whether with the Universe, with themselves or with others. Now that I coach other people, I feel much the same way. I want to win like any other coach and when people don't commit to winning in the greatest game of all, in their life, then why not get a little passionate about it. That passion will drive any coach to get better. But here's the thing that separates the great from the good coaches – can you still hold people in love and intention even if you are angry about their choices?

I started to feel the same way about commitment. I had three different people walk into my office within a few days, each asking if they could back out of their commitment. And what's crazy is that we are teaching our students to be more dedicated and more motivated. In fact, the last thing we say in every class is the fourth student creed: "We are a Black Belt school. We are dedicated, we are motivated, we're on a quest to be our best. We are aaaaaawesome!"

As part of our introductory lessons, we have the potential student kick as high as they can, which often exceeds what they believed they could, and then we ask them, "If I raised your goal higher, how many times would you try something before you give up?" The answer we're looking for, and that we want them to commit to is, 100 times. These people had verbally given me their commitment and by way of contract had given me their commitment and then to have them back out of their commitment, brought that same fiery emotion to the surface. I was starting to see why Jeff would get angry when people would choose not to get it.

I mentioned my experience to Jeff with the three families who wanted to back out of their karate agreements in a subsequent session and his take was a different one. He started to ask me if the experience was about me or about them. Was I coming from the thought of abundance – that each person had a different path to follow and that if one student left, another one or more would show up? Or was I coming from scarcity, where I needed each one of these students and I was afraid that if they left, I'd have less money to pay for rent and to keep the lights on?

Again, I had the opportunity to look at the challenge from another angle, and that angle was to see if the experiences with people were about me or about them or both. It's important to look at each situation by standing in your own shoes and asking, "Is this experience about me and if so, what can I learn from this? And then, standing in the other person's shoes and asking the same questions.

Taking a look at each situation from a different angle creates more empathy and more curiosity, creativity, love and ownership in your life. By asking these simple questions, I'm always learning and looking in the mirror of life to see how much I trust and love myself and how much curiosity and intention I can hold in what I want to become.

Feed The Dragon – Accept And Embrace Your Major Weakness

Because you've studied and lived your major weakness you're an expert at it. And when you teach how to overcome your weakness, you have mastered it.
– Jeff Allen

Now that I was more aware of my major weakness, I could hold myself more accountable, but through the vision of abundance, I could allow others to follow their own spiritual journey. I can be more raw and bold in my life.

There is an eastern philosophy that you have to accept the good and the evil, your strengths and your weaknesses before you can feel like a whole person. This expression is found in the ancient Yin Yang symbol; one being black and the other being white. It is a symbol that represents that in order to become a whole person, we have to come to accept everything, our weaknesses and our strengths, much the same way as each day includes both light and darkness.

In general, the Yin Yang symbol is a Chinese representation of the entire celestial phenomenon. It also contains the cycle of sun, the four seasons, 24-Segment Chi, the foundation of the I-Ching or Chinese philosophy and the Chinese calendar.

The Yin Yang symbol comes from observing the universe and the relationship between the sun and the moon. They called it the 'book of ease' or the 'book of changes.' The ancient Chinese people took an eight-foot pole, stuck it in the ground and observed how the sun and the shadows fell on the ground during the different seasons. By coloring in the darker areas to represent the time from the Summer Solstice to the Winter Solstice and the lighter part to represent the Winter Solstice to the Summer Solstice, the Yin Yang symbol appeared.

The light color indicates more sunlight, which is called Yang (Sun). The dark color area has less sunlight (more moonlight) and is called Yin (Moon). Yang is representative of the male. Yin is like the female. The Yin and Yang support each other and can't grow without each other. Yin couldn't give birth without Yang… joined together, making a whole circle – a circle of the universe, of time and season, and of life itself. (www.chinesefortunecalendar.com/yinyang.htm)

You can also consider the yin yang symbol to represent the two hemispheres of your brain. The yin is more spatial and flowing like your right brain and the yang is more direct and linear like your left brain. You can easily see how this topic of opposites continues to show up. And as part of the opposites, you will find a weakness.

Find your weakness, understand it, embrace it and let it teach you how to become better. You were given, or better yet, you chose a weakness, because it would teach you the path you should follow. Like Jeff said to me, and which another trainer taught him, "You can't know your purpose, unless you know your weakness."

Jeff said about your major weakness, "You must feed the dragon, not throw spears at it. This comes from the law of attraction. The more you try to throw spears at the dragon, the more fire comes back your way. The more you feed the dragon and make him your friend, the more you will be able to make him serve you. So if you have a weakness, a fault, a vice, or a sin that keeps coming back, see what it is trying to teach you. Ask yourself, 'How does this continue to serve my purpose and expansion?' You'll find that when it's served its purpose in teaching you, it will go away until you need to see it again to teach you another lesson. The dragon will teach you about you. Don't fear it, feed it and ask it life-learning questions. You don't defeat the dragon, you master it and it becomes one of your greatest life-long teachers."

Personal Wins for the Week

At the beginning of each coaching session I had with Jeff, he'd ask, "Tell me about your wins." At first I didn't know what he meant by wins. I'd learn quickly that wins were positive things that happened or new awareness that came through my conscious thoughts and choices. I would later find out that the wins were really a measuring device to Jeff and me about how I was progressing through the Intentional Vision process. Seeing and expressing my wins in life was part of the reprogramming that was going on in my mind. I started to see my challenges in a positive way and the positive things as miracles that I either co-created with my Creator or with my neighbors in life. Here are some of the wins I experienced in one particular week where I had several different interactions with people and with each I chose a different experience than I normally would have:

Using Affirmations – I created some large sticky notes with affirmations about my goals and I stuck them on my mirror in the bathroom. I also created some to put on the refrigerator door and on the wall next to my bed, so I could read them before I get up and before I go to bed.

I've also been using other affirmations to strengthen my intention in certain areas of my life. For instance, I've been saying, "I am the most inspiring karate instructor in the valley with the most life-changing program in the Rocky Mountains!" I felt this affirmation motivated me to really focus on the 'Word of the Week' this week. The 'Word of the Week' is a thought or concept I want to drive home with my students, so we are mentally challenging them to think about their lives and what's important. The Word of the Week was "Dreams". I asked my adult karate class, "What dreams did you have as a young child?" There were a few that pointed out that they were just what they wanted when they grew up. I pointed out to others that maybe they should take the feelings they were looking for in their childhood dreams and see if there are others dreams they can realize as adults, which give them the same feelings.

I'm finding that I'm having moments of discouragement. I almost think I'm pulling them up so I can test out my powers of affirmations. I've been fighting off the sense of illness. I've had my skin break out. I don't have the energy that I need. Yet, I still find myself using my affirmations more than before and it's making a difference in how I handle challenges that come up for me.

A Winning Interview – I interviewed one of Jeff's clients, who he described as, "a lady in her sixties, who really wanted to change and who worked really hard at it." She very recently graduated from the Intentional Vision coaching experience. I thought it was interesting that the most important things this lady learned was how to love herself, how to forgive herself and commune with her Creator, and how to empathize instead of sympathize. I learned from Jeff's student that she had a lot of Red in her personal identity, which made me realize that many of the emotions, growth, and awareness that happen to people in this experience, happen regardless of their personality traits. The one thing that this lady said that gave me goose bumps and sent an overwhelming sensation of warmth and peace through my body was, "For the first time since my childhood, I felt like a child. I felt connected to everyone and everything. I was curious about life and the world was a new place." Whoa! I felt the very same way, so to hear her say that validated my experience and helped me know that this was a normal sensation for everyone who really wants to have more and make more of their lives.

A Deeply Meaningful Moment With My Mother – I had the opportunity of learning more about that experience that help solidify my major weakness in my mind.

It wasn't until I was in high school and I had a fight with my mother that I found out how my grandmother died. I yelled at my mother and in exasperation, I said, "I hate my life, I should just go kill myself!" I went downstairs and plunked down in my bed. It wasn't more than 30 seconds later that my mother came down the stairs. She sat on the edge of my bed and I rolled away, so that I wouldn't have to face her. She had tears in her eyes, but she spoke very firmly. "Don't you ever say that again! Don't you ever say you'll kill yourself! My mother killed herself and it still hurts to this day to think about it!"

There have been times when my mother has talked just a little about my grandmother's death since that time. However, this week my mother came up and for the first time in a long time, I had a deep conversation with my mother and several of my sisters. I received a much better look at some of her pains and the fear and pain of her mother and her brothers – including how my grandmother killed herself. I had tears streaming down my face when she said, "My brother told my mother that he hated her and he wished she wasn't his mother. That was the day she killed herself. Can you imagine the pain my brother felt and still probably feels?"

My heart ached and went out to my mother and my uncles, who had to live with the pain of their mother's death. I finally understand even more why my mother chased me down into my room and told me, "Don't you ever say that again!" My love for my mother and my siblings grew that day and I attribute that in a way to being able to create a safe atmosphere – to trust myself and others – to talk about deep-seated feelings.

A Small Explosion To Learn From – On the other side of the emotional pendulum, I had a similar experience with my son getting very angry and blowing up at me. My oldest son is one of the leading youth on my SWAT (Super Winning Attitude Team) demonstration team. He was supposed to be working on a creative karate form with his team, but I could tell he wasn't putting in the effort. I've never really pushed my kids, because I don't want them to reject me or reject karate and all the good things they can learn from it.

I asked my son to practice using his nun-chucks, so he'd be able to help the team look better. He resisted and wanted to go play. I continued to ask him if he would just practice five or 10 minutes a day. I said, "Go get your chucks and we'll work on it right now." He very reluctantly grabbed his chucks. He did the nun-chuck form once and then wanted to go. I remained calm and encouraged him. I gave him a few things to work on, like swinging the chucks more with his wrist than with his arms. He repeated the form and looked worse. I said, "Come on son, I know you can do better than that. Do it one more time and then you can go." He picked his nun-chucks up and with a very intense, angry look on his face, he proceeded to do the form quite well. I was thinking to myself, "He should practice angry more often."

When my son was done, he threw his chucks down and went upstairs and slammed his bedroom door behind him. I'm not going to say that something inside of me snapped, because I really didn't lose it, but something happened to me. I went upstairs after him. I pushed open the door, which knocked him back a little. I could see the look of fear and defiance in his eyes. I got in his face and said, "I am not one to push you (ironically, I'd just about knocked him over by coming into the room), but right now your attitude stinks and it's affecting the way you're doing things. You're doing a disservice to yourself, to the team and to me!" My voice was raised and very firm, but everything in my mind was very clear. I hadn't lost it, like I've done a few times before. I was going to send the message loud and clear what I expected of him. "It comes down to your attitude. All I'm asking you to do is practice 10 to 15 minutes a day and you won't even do that!" I wanted to say, but didn't, "If you're going to go through life like that, you're not going to be anything but mediocre." As fast as that thought came to my mind, it disappeared with me as I walked out of the room.

I turned back around and said, "You know, I'm not your dad anymore at karate. I'm your coach and your teacher and maybe I need to push you more, because you don't seem to respond to me being a nurturing father when I'm at karate." Yes, I expressed myself with some emotion, but I felt I had done the right thing. I didn't feel guilty and I knew that maybe he needed a little fear motivation to wake him up. I said, "Son, it's up to you. I don't want you on the team if you're going to act like this or talk like you have. It's supposed to be a Super Winning Attitude Team and that's not you right now!"

My oldest son is really good about picking himself up and doing what he feels he needs to do. He turned into a different kid at karate and at home. Where he'd been a little bit aggressive with his mom and his brother and sisters, now he was being more helpful, like he's always been. I've also seen a little more drive in him at karate. I didn't mull over the conversation and beat myself up for it, like I would have done any other time. I did, however, go back in his room about 20 to 30 minutes later to ask him, "Are you all right?" I apologized for making him upset and I expressed why I felt the need to get after him. He also apologized.

Speaking Openly – My opportunities to exercise my communications skills continued to unfold this week. I had a very open and direct conversation with my assistant instructor, Mitch. Mitch had decided to stay in the valley and help me teach and build the school. You could tell that his whole demeanor had changed and that he had a new excitement for teaching.

It wasn't long before some of my adult students were making similar comments on how much Mitch seemed to care for all the students. He was acting the hero part and so many of my students looked up to him.

Mitch had expressed a desire to leave the studio, but wanted to continue training in some capacity with certain members of the martial arts system. However, he was afraid that because of expressing his desire to leave my studio, he'd offended the Master of the system and cut off any chance for continued training with them. I sat down with Mitch and assured him that the Master of the system wasn't offended; he simply wanted Mitch to hold up his side of his commitment to build the karate studio in our city. I told Mitch, "I'm going to see if we can continue having you go down to train with the group in their new Master's Club program." I could tell that Mitch knew I was on his side and wanted him to win in life. That simple look in his eye was a big win for me.

I'm gaining a greater vision of what is possible at my karate studio and how I can build my leadership team and improve my customer relations. I'm also feeling much more excited about teaching karate again. I can't say it enough how important it is to have a vision and know that it's possible to achieve! I also gained another six or seven students this last week and my numbers continue to climb. At this rate, I'll be able to get my head above the financial waters I've been buried in the last couple of years.

Making It Crystal Clear

1) The key to trusting yourself is knowing who you are and knowing your kryptonite – your major weakness or fear.

2) You will begin to trust yourself when you are willing to let things go and forgive yourself.

3) Faith and intention are about seeing your potential and the possibilities in life.

4) You must own and embrace your kryptonite – it's a part

of you so live like you chose it and wanted it to teach you about life and love – so feed the dragon.

Intentional Vision Exercises

1) Who in your life really needs to hear from you that you love them?

2) Look to see what your major weakness is. Write down all the bad things that have happened to you; sickness, deaths, divorce, separations or calamities. Fill in the chart on the next page – examples show how different events elicit different feelings but when peeled back, the underlying emotion or fear is still the same. This underlying emotion is your kryptonite factor. With the list of problems, failures, and calamities listed in the first column, write the negative emotion you were feeling at the time of the event, then ask the question several times over, "What is the emotion under that one?" and write the answers in the third and fourth columns. Eventually you'll arrive at your major weakness. You may need to ask someone else to help you look at it as well. A friend or good 'neighbor' will often be the one to point out what's not obvious to you. Many times a friend or family member is the best person to help you see what you couldn't previously see about yourself.

3) Continue to write down what makes you happy and the wins you had this week. Share a win with someone close to you.

4) Have a close friend or family member review some of your findings to confirm what you've discovered about your major weakness. Have your friend or family member help you explore whether there are any other emotions that underpin the ones you've listed.

Major Crisis or Tragedy in Life	What Was the Emotion or Fear Tied to the Crisis or Tragedy?	What Was the Emotion or Fear Under That?	What Was the Emotion or Fear Under That?
Example: Breakup With Girlfriend/Boyfriend	Sadness and Confusion	Feeling Inadequate	Fear of Not Being Good Enough
Example: Death of Close Family Member	Guilt for Being Alive When He/She Died	Wonder if I Did Enough to Show Love	Fear of Not Being Good Enough

Chapter 5

Trust That Your Neighbor Is Also A Superhero

We two form a multitude.
– Ovid

    I remember as a Boy Scout being asked by my dad, who was one of the scout leaders, to call the local fire department. I was supposed to see if our troop could go check out the fire station. Instead I sat by the phone for what seemed like hours wishing the fire department would call me. I even dialed the number and after a few rings, I hung up. I just couldn't do it. I wanted to go to the fire station and see the fire engines and maybe slide down the pole and wear the fireman's hat, but I couldn't bear calling a stranger and asking them for something. I never made the call, no matter how many times I picked up the phone. I never found out what it would be like to be a hero like a fireman. I procrastinated long enough that some other scouting activity came up and superseded the one I was supposed to lead. I still remember that time because I've relived it many times throughout my life when I've failed to make the call I should have made. Why couldn't I have just made the call? Now I know I had a sub-conscious pattern running in my mind preventing me from communicating my desires to the people who could help me the most.

Up until going through this Intentional Vision course, I can easily say that I'd much rather speak before a group of people I don't know than speak one-on-one with someone I didn't know. I'd often shift my gaze from people's eyes and look away, so I didn't catch their attention or have to talk to them. It wasn't comfortable for me to talk to someone I didn't know and the conversations would often feel stinted and forced. I most certainly didn't trust others and myself before my new awareness.

In a conversation, not only did I fret over everything before I said it, which leads to more fear of being rejected or fear of offending, or fear of looking stupid, but I'd also rather sit and stew over everything I said in the conversation. I'm always rethinking conversations I've had and wondering why I didn't say something right or how I could have said something better and with more feeling. I used to live in fear of communicating my feelings and needs, which always stood in the way of being the best at what I was doing.

When I first met Jeff Allen, I had just walked into a conference room. I sat down so I could look out the 6th floor windows at the expansive lake that joined with the mountains on the horizon. I was the first one from my product management and marketing team there and before they entered, a sharp looking fellow with a big smile greeted me. It was Jeff. I wasn't sure what to say to the guy. I always felt uncomfortable around new people on a one-on-one basis. So I was glad when many of my corporate teammates began to show up.

Jeff looked like he could have been an executive or a friendly salesman by his smile. He turned out to be both; a leader and a big closer. It didn't take long before Jeff had removed my defenses and he seemed like an old friend I was excited to meet each week. As I began my journey through the Intentional Vision process with Jeff, I had a feeling he was going to teach me something new about myself and about my life. One of the first lessons I connected with was how to develop Co-Creative communications.

I remember associating the Co-Creative communications with the win-win philosophy I had first learned from Stephen Covey. And sometimes Jeff would also refer to this as co-creating a winning relationship. However, this time when I went through the one-on-one training I continued to marvel at how deep I'd dive into this principle.

The 3rd Law of Intentional Vision – Trust Your Neighbor Is Also A Superhero
(Week 4 Reading Assignment)

Trust each other again and again. When the trust level gets high enough, people transcend apparent limits, discovering new and awesome abilities for which they were previously unaware.
– David Armistead

Call it homework, call it Intentional Vision exercises, whatever you call it – we hope you're doing it! By repeatedly doing your homework on a daily basis you will be building a new neural-network in your brain to break old, negative patterns of thinking. Otherwise, you continue to do what you have always done, somehow expecting a different outcome – a good definition of insanity.

Now that you trust the Universe has what you want and you trust yourself enough to go get it, you likely have an inner feeling of extra confidence. Your confidence will be exposed to others as courage to be great. You will be constantly thinking about, "How can I accomplish my desires and who can I ask to help?"

The next step is to trust that others are superheroes who are willing and able to help you. At this level of trust, you cannot trust others if you don't trust yourself. The level of trust you have in yourself will reflect in the level of trust others have in you. If your level of commitment to yourself is low, then the people in your life will mostly be fair-weather friends and not the really committed kind.

When you get to this level of effort it is important to know that you can't do it on your own. You really need to establish a team that has a shared best interest at heart. And when you have a team that you trust, you have that extra wind in your sails. You will be on the go, creating and maintaining winning relationships.

The fact of the matter is, if you are fear-motivated in relationships, then you are also afraid to trust yourself. Fear is quickly exposed in relationships. Often, fear micromanages the environment in constant judgment, so that no one can feel trust. Fear may also expose itself by never fully communicating within your relationships, or not helping your relationships be the best they can be. This lack of trust creates an environment that is always minimizing the potential of the human spirit.

If you want to enjoy the journey of life, it requires a team, a team with different responsibilities and talents. When sharing the journey with a talented team, your efforts will be much easier and your rewards will be much greater – not only financially, but in every aspect of your life.

It is important to point out here that it is nearly impossible for someone else to do all the work and give you the credit. So you need to be a workhorse and encourage them to be a workhorse too. It takes action to fully experience the benefits of your intentions. And the best way for others to understand your level of commitment, trust, and passion is to share the 9 Laws of Intentional Vision to create and experience greater love and freedom.

Now you may be asking, "What about those who I have trusted and I either got burned by or ended up on the short end of the stick?" I'm sure you have had a business partner or a personal relationship who totally abused you or dumped their troubles on you. And it may seem like the person is a thief or a bully, but remember that everything has a purpose. If you *let go and let God*, you will learn why this 'lesson' was attracted into your life. And if you own it and study it, you'll begin to see that you asked for the experience. I know that can be a hard pill to swallow (it is for anyone at first), but remember that the Universe is always in fair exchange. The lessons you receive are ones you requested for your own learning purposes.

Life is all about a spiritual learning and if love is the most dominate power governing our existence, then the only way love can be truly experienced is through self agency, or the ability to choose one's level of success. It is through teaching and living at this level of ownership and accountability, that others can achieve their inner desire without ridicule and judgment.

At this level of awareness it is important to understand how to hold self-value or self-worth. Experiencing worthy is when you feel safe, trust, and love. To be worthy, you need to interpret past learning experiences as a means to evaluate your future success, and not a method to devalue or beat up on yourself.

All of life's lessons are a divine method to teach us how to increase in love and self-agency in all areas of our life experience. It is now time to trust yourself enough that when issues get heated or tough, you are able to remain calm, clear, and concise by knowing who you are. In fact, our innate programming wants more of these 'life lessons' so much that it is always driving us to achieve. These life lessons are commonly providing us the learning tools/lessons that some call a bad experience. But in truth, you asked for your specific lesson, because it is the best way for you to gain the wisdom you need.

To overcome past negative learning and pursue your dreams in a healthy way you must trust your ability to be raw with yourself. Learn why you needed this lesson. It is time to trust yourself enough that when issues get heated or tough you are able to remain calm, clear, and concise through knowing who you are.

Without the ability to know yourself and trust yourself, you give all power and decision-making abilities over to someone else by conforming to their needs. This is unhealthy conforming. There is healthy conforming that is good, like helping with daily responsibilities and obeying traffic laws. But then there is unhealthy conforming which is like a sickness that takes away the love, passion and purpose from your life. Unhealthy conforming removes the "feel good" emotion, because it is the same as living a lie, but the difference is, we are lying to ourselves. We are telling ourselves that it is okay to be untrue.

Simply said, stay away from emotional vampires. Stay away from anyone or anything that overcomes your positive desires, causing you to conform in an unhealthy way. Some relationships might start with simple differences, but then escalate into large differences. You continue to give in all the time, hoping they will become easier to get along with. You want them to be as fair as you have been, but in reality you end up a victim and taken advantage of by another emotional vampire.

Most of us have been taught as a child to conform to get along and be accepted. But many times the way we are conforming only allows us to experience how to be a victim, a victim that is in conflict with our personal goals and desires.

Victim energy is a choice and a hard way to learn how to succeed. A victim blames other events and people they feel have cheated them or not given them a fair shot. They are a victim and will remain one until they either take their final 'dirt nap' or have a change of attitude.

Well the time for being a victim has ended! Your time is now! It's time to take advantage of this law and start asking people to help you with your goals and desires and make your goals shared goals, so that you will become free; to be free the way you were meant to be, where you can do anything you desire, anytime you want to. You know the feeling… where you have no fear and the world seems to be at your fingertips, where everything seems to magically fall into place just as you intended it. It is also important that you do not become an emotional vampire to others and take advantage of their wellbeing. Instead, you need to support their goals, so they can be of assistance to your goals.

There is a divine energy inside you declaring that you deserve the most love that life has to offer. You deserve to be free.

Remember, what you see is what you get and what you have is what you saw.

It is you, and only you, who will ever be able to change your life. Great things happen to great people, because they see greatness in others and are attracting great people to the great things they are doing. The people who win in life are anxiously engaged in inviting others to be on their team. Those who succeed in life develop a way to help others become successful. You become successful because you coach, mentor, and teach as many people as needed to help your team win.

In life, the foundation for successful people is trust. You must first have a clear understanding that trust is healthy for everyone involved. This level of trust cannot be motivated by fear; it must be motivated by love, gratitude, abundance, and the ability to see potential possibilities. This trust must also encourage others to be able to trust the environment. Make sure it is not false hope; find the people you can trust.

You have heard the term "Success breeds success." This means that once you help others succeed, you will in turn succeed. In other words, start by getting good people on your team and then help them become as successful as possible.

Your real job is to be the breeder of success. For example, if you want to start a fine dining restaurant, you need a great chef. And the best way to find a great chef is to start asking a lot of the right people – put it out to the Universe. As you are asking, you maintain a deep level of trust that everyone is helping you find the right person.

Then when you find the right person and put them on the team, you start the process of making them successful. You will work hard and long to help them become the most successful chef possible, and in return you can begin to see what it is doing for your restaurant. The quality and consistency of your meals keep customers coming back for more and sharing with other people. One of the great perks of staying true to the laws that govern freedom is in the event that one of your team members chooses to no longer be a good team player (they lost your trust), you are still able to trust that the Universe has someone else, and trust yourself to go find that person. Your level of stress to change team members is not fearful or dramatic, because you know the Universe has so many good people who want to help you – especially if you are willing to help them become successful.

If you are coaching to win and playing to win in your game, you will succeed. Again, success breeds success, and if you are not on a team, it will be nearly impossible to achieve your deserved level of freedom.

So…do your Intentional Vision exercises and look for your wins!

How Do You Play The Superhero or Victim Game?

In a controversy the instant we feel anger we have already ceased striving for the truth, and have begun striving for ourselves.
—Buddha

Jeff pointed to his bookshelf and said, "There are plenty of books written about the next topic, but let's integrate them into one concept of how to play to win."

He continued, "How do people play their lives? There are basically four different positions from which people play their lives. There's play to win, play not to lose, just play, and not play at all."

Play Not To Lose – Win/Lose – So let's describe the people who play not to lose first, because that's what the majority of people do. For instance, there is a joke about a momma bear that comes tearing out of the woods after two campers. One of the men sits down on the ground to put his running shoes on. The other guy looks back and asks, "Why are you putting your running shoes on? You can't outrun the bear." The man putting the shoes on replies, "I don't have to outrun the bear, I only have to outrun you!" and that's playing not to lose.

Let's put some relationship positioning into that same playing not to lose concept. That would be a win/lose relationship. As long as the bear doesn't eat me, I'm okay if he gets you. If I'm not playing to win, then I'm not playing to lose. You've seen it happen in any sport when a team has a big lead and then they start playing to protect their lead and play not to lose. That is when the other team gains the momentum and wins the game. When the team focuses on the opponent, because that's who they have to conquer, then they are playing not to lose. But if the team focuses on doing their best and scoring more points and the fundamentals of scoring more points, then they will have far more victories.

Those who are playing not to lose are driven by the emotion that "I'm okay and you're not okay." In other words, all you need is a good pair of running shoes or a competitive edge on your neighbor and you will win and who cares if the bear ate the other guy.

Just Play – Lose/Win – If we play not to lose we are in a win/lose relationship, but if we are just playing to be in the game, we are in a lose/win relationship. And those who are willing to just play are willing to simply be accepted on the team and they're willing to lose with the team if they're accepted. They are simply not making an attempt at winning and they live the phrase, "Misery loves company." They will pull everyone down to their level of self-destruction.

Then there are those who just play, who are driven by the emotion of, "You're okay and I'm not okay." These are the individuals that never seem to speak their mind. They go along to get along. They wait patiently, hoping for acceptance and love, believing that if they wait long enough, they will eventually win.

Play to Lose – Lose/Lose – Those who are not playing at all are in a lose/lose situation. There are also the individuals who play to lose who are driven by the emotion of, "I'm not okay and I don't want you to be okay." You can see how this group ends up not winning. In fact, for them, losing is winning as long as they can drag others down to their position.

Play to Win – Win/Win – Now there are the ones who play to win. And they play to win by helping others win and gathering like-minded people onto their team. They truly have a genuine interest in helping others accomplish their goals and in turn the relationship is in a state that they know they are also going to win. This is because the other person is also working hard to help them accomplish their goals. As you can see, both individuals have full disclosure of how each individual wants to win and each makes a concerted effort to share the victory helping them win. If you are experiencing the win with others, you are in a win/win situation.

In those situations where we play to win by focusing on our goal (score more points), our performance will far exceed what we could do if we play not to lose, because our emotions are attached to the goal of winning. You can see that this program was taught to us and is running in our imprinted mind and doesn't serve our purpose of winning in life. When we're running this scarcity program, we believe there needs to be a win/lose relationship in all areas of our life. You will always be protecting yourself from not losing and that's a sure way not to win. When you're focusing on the negative and not to lose, you will be sure to attract more losses into your life. It's just like a bicycle; it goes the same direction you're looking.

The person who plays to win is driven by the emotion of "I'm okay and you're okay", having a full understanding and trust that both parties are healthy and engaged in the game to win.

The Vicious Parent-Child-Victim Triangle

Jeff said, "Why don't we take another look at how these positions play out by giving them some roles." He drew a big circle on the board with an "X" through it. He then filled in the titles of "Co-Creator, Parent, Child and Victim" on the whiteboard. Of all the diagrams of principles I remembered during my first leadership training with Jeff, the Co-Creator-Parent-Child-Victim diagram is the easiest to call to memory. 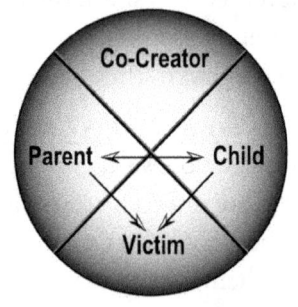 It is also the easiest one to recognize in action. However, creating adult communications and relationships instead of falling into the Parent-Child-Victim behavior triangle is not as easy as it is to recognize. It's like learning a foreign language, where it's much easier to understand the language than to actually speak it, understanding and recognizing each role is easier than living it. The biggest reason is that these patterns for relationships and communications come from the subconscious mind and are habitual.

Parent/Child Relationships – Listen to almost any conversation and you can pick out a few roles people play by how they speak to others. The first is the Parent, the "I'm okay and you're not okay," person. This is the person telling others what to do, how to do it, and what they need to know. It's an authoritative voice that can be very judgmental in nature. The Parent role takes charge of any conversation by whatever means he or she can. The Parent tends to think ahead in the conversation and try to outdo the other person with their knowledge or response. They have to be in charge, they have to win no matter what – because to them, not winning or feeling important would be losing. Think of a time you took on the Parent role. What happened?

The second role is that of the Child, "You're okay, I'm not okay," which is played by those who are always taking advice or listening to someone who has taken on a role of superior knowledge. They often just do what the Parent tells them to do, but it's often done with a certain amount of resentment. They will only do something when they are told to do it. The Parent/Child relationship is symbiotic. One thrives on the other. This relationship doesn't just exist in a family relationship. It exists everywhere – between a manager and a worker, between a coach and his or her players, between anyone putting himself or herself higher than another as would an expert.

Occasionally, the Parent/Child communication is necessary. This is certainly true in an emergency, such as someone getting hurt and a person telling someone else to "Call 9-1-1!" or to get out of a burning building or within a military organization. Maybe a person of authority making an emergency decision may have to play the Parent role to help a company recover from a disaster.

However, the Parent/Child relationship in a society that seeks "life, liberty and the pursuit of happiness" doesn't make sense if we want to explore our true personal or social potential. Instead, the Parent/Child relationship will often result in the Child role turning into the Victim role, which is the "I'm not okay and I hope I can make you not okay." This role of the victim is one of fear and weakness. Here is where people tend to go if held too long in a Parent/Child relationship. The Victim feels powerless to change and much of life's joy seems stolen away by those playing the Parent role. The only problem with this role, as with all the roles, is that it is a chosen role. All you have to do is listen to someone go on and on about all the bad things that have happened to him or her. You'll be able to tell that they have chosen this role and in many ways they get some kind of satisfaction from it. On the other hand, you can listen to another person talk about all the challenges they've faced in life and know that they are not a victim; they've overcome their challenges, they own their experience.

The Parent role can also move to a victim position when they feel guilty for things they've said or how they've said it. Think of a parent who gets very angry with their child and then feels like they're a bad parent afterwards. The same is true of any other relationship where the person who is aggressively commenting with their "greater" knowledge and then feels like they've offended the other person.

Can you list at least three people who seem to always be playing in the Parent-Child-Victim mode? Describe your current relationship with a few different people and see how you are playing your game.

Playing Victim – The Victim is a lower level of the Parent-Child and is what either the Parent or the Child evolves into when he or she feels they're trapped in a certain role. The Victim will detract from any communication or activity. They are always caught up in backbiting, creating rumors, and finding fault with others. The Victim is very judgmental of everything and feels that everyone is out to get them. They often blame God or the Universe for being aligned against them. They wallow in self-pity and are attracted to people who feel sorry for them. The Victim detracts or diminishes from the value of any group. The Victim is primarily motivated by fear and a sense of scarcity. If caught in a Victim mode for too long, people trend toward depression and in severe cases, they may even take their own life.

Who do you know that is playing victim in their life? How do you feel when you're around this person? What would it take for this person to break out of their current pattern of thought?

Parent-Child-Victim Process – It's important to note that all of these patterns are imprinted on us in our early childhood. And the patterns are running to tell us that if we want to win, someone else needs to lose. So the question is, are we running our lives or are the patterns in our brains running our lives?

Jeff gave an example of the Parent-Child-Victim playing out, "Let's take the traditional process in marriage. Two people get married and the husband decides that he's going to play the Parent role and take charge and that the wife is going to play the Child role and follow his lead. So right from the beginning, they are not equal in their relationship. At some point, the woman wakes up and says to herself, 'I'm not going to take it any more. He's an idiot and he's made so many mistakes. Why have I been allowing him to make all these mistakes? I'm going to take charge.'"

The first thought that came to mind when Jeff told this story was something that happened during the first year of my marriage. I was in charge of our personal finances and I would keep a running total of my checking account in my head. I knew how much I had in the bank and I knew what checks I'd written. I'd only bounced one check in my life and that was when I rented the tuxedos for our wedding. I made a deposit the very next day before we flew off to Hawaii for our honeymoon.

At the time, I had a good idea when we went into that first holiday season as a newlywed couple as to how much money we had in the bank. When my wife started to spend a bunch of money on presents, I jumped on her case. I remember exactly where we were standing in the local mall when I chastised her for spending too much on presents and I made her take one of them back. I was playing the Parent role perfectly in that holiday moment. With a broken spirit and a dejected look, she took back the present.

"The imprinted or subconscious mind is running this game - it's not the conscious or intending mind." Jeff continued with the example of the married couple, "So the imprinted mind engages to no longer play the Child role and uses the same tools it was taught when engaging with her parents to feel okay. In order to feel okay, the imprinted mind asks, 'How did I take charge and win the last time I did this with my parents? Well, my parents said I couldn't have something and I started screaming and I got my way.' But the husband who is acting as the parent has been trained that if he gets screamed at, he screams back. Now you've got two people running imprinted programs at the same time and in both cases the programs are saying, 'I'm going to win no matter what it takes!' (I'm okay and you're not okay.) And these programs will continue to run off and on until they either get a divorce and go their own way or the pain gets to be too great and the intending mind of the husband or wife comes in and starts asking the question, 'Wait a minute, this is idiotic! This is too painful!' The point is, the parent/child program will continue to run, forcing you to be a victim or until you start using your intending mind to communicate and play the Co-Creative role."

My thoughts drifted back to who now controls our finances in my marriage. It wasn't very long after the holiday mall incident that my wife came to me and said, "I hate not knowing how much money we have in our account. You have an idea, but I don't. I want to take over the checkbook. I'll always keep it in balance and we'll always know how much we can spend." She wasn't kicking and screaming, like Jeff was saying. Instead she was using her "teal" personality to persuade me with facts and reason until I conceded the checkbook to her.

Jeff tied this behavior back to the personalities by saying, "Based on what personality you have, the intending mind will start to say there is too much pain and will give in to the innate mind. The intending mind tried, but it was too painful. Now the innate mind takes over and starts operating in a fear-based, scarcity mode. If you're mostly Red, you'll attack. If you're Blue, you'll run away. If you're Orange, you'll keep yelling. If you're Yellow, you'll yell and then acquiesce. If you're Teal, you'll use logic and facts from the past. And if you're Green, you'll shut up and fold your arms in defiance." I realized that I had done the "Blue" thing and ran away from financial discussions with my wife. And now if there are any money problems, the reverse of the mall scene plays out. I'm the one that is usually standing by getting scolded, feeling like a problem child.

Jeff really made me sit back and wonder about how much I own my experience. Am I running my brain or is my brain running me? Jeff continued, "However long this battle goes, it doesn't matter. At some point, someone is going to end up in the Victim mode and start blaming the other. At all levels of consciousness the idea of the other person being at fault resonates." Think of a time when you felt like a child or a victim. How did it feel and how often do you feel this way? You can choose a different experience.

Taking 100% Responsibility – Jeff then said something that I had heard him say a few times before, but this time I was really getting the meaning. "The problem is that no one is willing to step back and say, 'I'm 100% responsible for this conversation.' They've never heard that pattern in their entire life. But the, 'I'm 100% responsible for this conversation' is really the first step back toward a more Co-Creative interaction. If you think about our couple that is arguing, they're both 100% responsible for the entire interaction."

Jeff continued, "The person who started the conversation is 100% responsible. And if the other person says the next word, then they are 100% responsible for the interaction, whatever it is, good or bad."

"Whatever the results of the heated interaction, one or both people end up playing the victim role. Eventually, the husband says to himself, consciously, 'This is stupid, I'm going to patch things up and try going about this in a different way (Child role).'"

"So the husband goes and patches things up and asks for forgiveness, and she says, 'That's right, that's what I'm talking about! It's going to be different now.' She then takes charge of the situation. After a while with the wife running the show, the husband slips into the child role and may eventually slip into the victim mode, so that the cycle repeats itself. When the process and programs repeat, it soon becomes a vicious triangle. You could call it a love-hate triangle, but many times it turns out to be more of a victim triangle, because no matter what, someone ends up feeling like a victim. Everyone in the relationship takes turns being either a parent, child or victim."

I asked Jeff how a statement he said earlier, "You can't feel justice while you're being a judge," fit with this example.

Jeff perked up even more and leaned forward in his chair. He held his hands up as if I'd scored a touchdown or a three-point shot. "That's right! That's why this example exists. Everyone is being a judge and no one feels justice. Whenever you put someone else in a different place or at a different level than yourself, you are judging them. You're labeling them as something different than yourself, because in your mind you're superior in your thinking."

At the time, this little conversation about judging others didn't have its full impact on me. It wasn't until months later that I'd gain an even greater awareness of being in a state of judgment and how it places us in different roles to play instead of coming at a challenge with the feeling that everyone can win and everyone has something to learn and teach. In essence, judging others is placing your self agency in front of others and goes against the idea of the need to experience self agency or choice in life.

I'm Okay, You're Okay – By now, Jeff was up and moving around. The room was too small for his enthusiasm and he obviously was in the coaching zone, because he really wanted me to get this idea. He said, "But let's say that the person playing the Child role comes screaming at the other person and the person stops and asks, 'Where's the justice in this situation? Let me understand what you need and let's see if we can find something that is fair for you and fair for me.' You can see that once one person enlists the other person in looking for a fair solution – something that will be a win for both – the fight goes away."

Jeff lifted one hand higher than the other like he was tipping the scales to one side and he shifted his attention to how the Co-Creative role works. "The whole Co-Creative experience is that it comes from a place of, 'I'm okay and you're okay.' It is more of an observer role than someone who is so tied up in their emotional patterns and just lets their programs run. Because if you don't have a belief that says, 'You're a good person – I wouldn't have married you unless I thought you were a good person. And I'm a good person too. We're good people and we make a good team if we choose to,' then you can't step back and say, 'Let's stop looking at this as, you're different than me. Let's look at it as, you're okay and I'm okay. In this new Co-Creative experience it takes a higher level of commitment to love – not the romantic love – love in the manner of respect, honor, cherishing, commitment, humility, or the love toward your neighbor kind of love."

Jeff pointed to his bookshelf. "In a biblical sense, 'love your neighbor as yourself' is the same thing as 'I'm okay, you're okay'. If a person cannot stand in front of the mirror and say, 'I love myself,' then it's guaranteed that they are stuck in the Parent-Child-Victim triangle." This was my first insight into the fact that life is a mirror, and the way we treat ourselves, within our own minds, is the way we'll inevitably treat others. If we don't trust ourselves, we won't trust others.

I wanted Jeff to reiterate what he'd just said, so I asked, "So I go off and run through your Intentional Vision process and if I find it really difficult to do my affirmations like 'I love myself and I play to win,' then I'm probably stuck in this triangle?"

"There's no probably about it!" I could tell Jeff was very serious about this point, but he was still smiling as if he'd scored the winning shot in a game. This time he spoke slowly to make the point even clearer. "If you don't have respect and love for self, sufficient enough to put another person on your same level, then you ARE stuck in this victim triangle!" There was a tone of certainty that resonated in his voice. "If you don't have self-respect and self-love, then you're in judgment. The more you search for justice within this victim triangle, the more unjust it will seem and the more confused you'll get about your experience. There's no resolution in judgment – it's an endless loop."

As I've witnessed other people with the challenges in marriage and my own challenges – of being in judgment – this is the biggest reason for being stuck within a relationship. Not coming at challenges as a Co-Creative person, with an, "I'm okay, you're okay" or "Win-Win" attitude, is the foundation of every power struggle in a relationship.

Another example Jeff gave me was that of a person who forgets to put gas in their car and then down the road runs out of gas. "Now the person has a few choices to make. Justice was served by his running out of gas, or we could say that he suffered the consequences. Now if this happened to us, what would we say to ourselves? 'I'm an idiot!' (Parent/Child) or we could cast the blame on someone else. 'If I hadn't received that phone call from my neighbor, I wouldn't have forgotten to stop at the gas station!' (Victim) or 'What can I learn from this new situation? Or I wonder how it will benefit me in the end?'" (Co-Creator).

As Jeff was settling back into his chair, I threw out the idea that we are working on our own "love" triangle when we are saying 'I love myself and I play to win!' The affirmations you say help you break the conversational habits you have with yourself, so that you can break those same habits outside yourself. When you can step outside yourself with an awareness to see a parent-child interaction happening and then change it around, your life changes.

Jeff smiled and nodded to acknowledge my observation and said, "I used to have people say, 'I love myself, I like myself,' like the first time you went through this program. Now I have people say, 'I love myself and I play to win,' because the whole Co-Creative experience is really a 'Play to Win' experience. Play to win means you are looking for the positive wins in your life."

Jeff made it clear that there are times when you have to play the parent. "If the house is on fire, you have to tell everyone to GET OUT!"

I chuckled and said, "Yeah, it wouldn't make much sense to stop and ask your child, 'How do you feel about your clothes catching on fire?'"

I think Jeff caught the image, laughed and said, "No, when your kid's pants are on fire, that's not the time to ask him what he's learning from this experience either. You have to play the Parent at times." Jeff continued the thought, "Another good word for Parent within the business world is the 'Boss'. This is not the same as a manager who uses a Co-Creative conversation, which would augment the work environment. The manager who uses a Co-Creative management style will achieve far greater productivity than any other style of management. But sometimes when you're the Boss and the others want to play the Apprentice (Child) role, you have to make it clear that they are not getting their work done or that they're not accomplishing what they need to. It's okay to be the Boss sometimes, as long as the employees have had the training and know what is expected of them."

Jeff leaned back and spread his arms out, acting like he was sizing something up. He then gave a great metaphor for looking at the Parent or Boss in business. "I like to represent any business as a ship. The ship is in the middle of the ocean and it has to make it to shore for everyone on the ship to survive. Now if there's someone on the ship that is keeping it from getting to shore, you better get him off the ship! You don't have much of a choice. It's not so much that you chose, but that they chose. It's the idea of choice and consequences. If you're choosing to throw them off and didn't train them how to trim the sails or to navigate the boat, then it's your fault."

Jeff looked up at the ceiling, smiled as if he'd remembered something and looked back at me. "The other interesting thing about the business as a ship scenario is the amount of money that is flowing through the business." He held his arms out in front of him, "It's like the wind that fills the sails. The more money that flows, the more the wind blows and the happier everyone is and the more love there is in the boat. If there's no money flowing – there's no wind – then everyone on that boat is irritable and ornery and there is plenty of fear in the boat."

Jeff quickly took me back to the idea of the Co-Creator role and said, "This principle of creating Co-Creative relationships is a huge key to success. It's the idea that if we come together in some interaction, the results may not be perfect, but the fact that I can say, 'You're an awesome person, regardless of anything that has happened,' is important. In fact, to me, *this one principle of being able to go out into the world both as an observer and a participant creates more awareness than almost anything else taught in this Intentional Vision process.*"

Co-Creative Conversations

> *We can easily forgive a child who is afraid of the dark;*
> *the real tragedy of life is when men are afraid of the light.*
> – Plato

Where do we pick up all these patterns that make us victims in life? Well it's just part of the process of life and it seems to be designed for a purpose – the purpose of understanding the difference between love and fear. We develop the patterns out of fear to protect us from the pain we experience through our major weakness. We follow those patterns because we mistakenly think that if we avoid the pain, we'll have happiness. Happiness is not about avoiding the pain.

Jeff shifted his swiveling executive chair to face the whiteboard to look at what was drawn on it. The board was full of circles and arrows. He swiveled back to me and said, "You might ask yourself, how do we teach or give our children this program."

"Which program is that?" I asked.

"The program of learning the difference between love and fear," he replied. "I think it is part of this whole mortal experience. It was planned from the beginning." Jeff continued to explain using the Bible as an example, you have the Old Testament, which is mostly related to a God of fear, where God's people showed that they weren't ready for a higher law (much like a young child), so they were given very strict laws and if they disobeyed the law, there was a heavy penalty. In the New Testament, when Christ came among men, He showed a higher law and a greater example of love. The rest of the New Testament is about Christ's followers working out their spiritual growth and understanding through both love and fear."

This Biblical love and fear process relates very closely to our lives and how we grow and mature in all aspects – within our minds, in accordance with our bodies, and to the depths of our spirits. As Jeff put it, "We go through fear. We gain a better understanding about love. And then we work out the rest of our life in love and fear. You see we can't understand love fully until we understand fear. We have to go through this process of being raised by a parent who says, 'Don't do that!', 'Do this!', 'No that is wrong!', 'You're bad if you do this!' or 'You're good if you do that!'…which puts limits on our lives. This is so we can get fear figured out. Without this experience, we wouldn't be able to fully understand and experience love."

I'm pondering this idea as I'm writing Jeff's words out. I first thought, "What about an infant who can feel the close attachment and love coming from his parents while they cradle him or her in their arms?" Then it struck me that we need to experience love at all levels of our life, within each level of our personalities. It's then that we can experience love in an intentional state – in a state of creation, or co-creation with God. That state of creation can be in your mind or in your relationships. It can even be in a simple conversation that creates a greater understanding.

Jeff continued, "The number one blocking program that people experience in communications is that of, 'how do I get my topic, emotions, and energy across to another person?' When we are trapped in this experience of fear, we either get trapped in the Child experience where we say, 'What do I need to do to get along? I'm not going to talk.' Or you're going to take the Parent position and beat the person down with your opinions. Then they get trapped in the Victim triangle and their experience remains in fear and worry. The people who get this and decide to implement this one concept of breaking out of the Victim triangle have enormous growth through this Intentional Vision process."

I could easily relate to this experience. As a Blue person, I used to think it was really important to get across what I had to say and that speaking was the only way to communicate. I would worry about every word I said and I'd often review each important conversation after the fact and find all the areas where I screwed up. This type of fear doesn't lend itself to good communications. Now after gaining a greater awareness, I often communicate more from the heart, listen with the heart and enjoy the communication and connection. Every conversation is a perfect one because I believe it's there to teach me something. I just let the conversation stand as is and let it be what it will, without forcing any issues. It's fun to sit back and be the observer as you participate in connections with someone you care about.

Jeff mentioned how his clients often talk about their wins. "People will come back with their wins in breaking out of the Victim triangle and say, 'Wow! I got into this confrontation and I took a moment to step back and say, How can I help this person win? Then I went back into that experience and it was so simple and it turned out better than I expected.' That is how the Co-Creator wins, he or she steps back and asks a few questions like, 'Am I really playing in my game?, Is this person in the same game?, or How can I help you win?' These simple questions bring up all sorts of interesting solutions.

Additional questions that come up from the Co-Creator position include, 'What is it that I need to win and is this person in the same game as I am?' If the other person isn't in the same game, then it becomes easy to say, 'I don't need to play with you right now because we're not in the same game together.' You can easily let go of any situation once you've stepped back as the observer and asked yourself the Co-Creative questions."

Jeff identified that whether you're talking about a monetary-related or time-related exchange in your life, you still have to identify if you are serving purpose. "It's all about finding and serving your purpose, which is the ultimate goal of this Intentional Vision program you're going through. Why would you take your time to go off to this person's purpose, unless it serves your purpose?"

Co-Creative vs. Parent-Child-Victim Relationships

Words are just words and without heart they have no meaning.
  – Chinese proverb

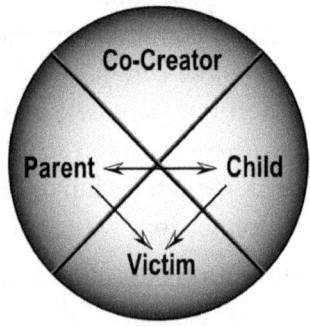

As Jeff approached the topic of Co-Creative relationships, I thought to myself, "Although it's none of my business and I shouldn't be concerned what others think about me, if I really want to influence people, share my feelings, and change the world in some way, I have to get in the game and communicate."

So how do we communicate with others? Many times we communicate with others in much the same way we communicate with ourselves. If we tend to beat up on ourselves, then we'll end up doing the same to others. If we treat ourselves like victims then we'll fall victim to others.

People get stuck in their relationships because they have allowed a Parent/Child/Victim triangle to develop. No one in a Parent/Child/

Victim relationship is sharing their needs, desires, or their innermost feelings. As I spent more time with Jeff discussing the Parent/Child/Victim relationship, it hit me like a revelation that this same Victim triangle often develops within the walls of our own head. I have often held a conversation like this with myself: "(Parent) Why did you say that? That was kind of stupid. (Child) I don't know why I do things like that. (Victim) I must be stupid, why can't I ever get it right? I'd be better off not saying anything." Can you hear these roles playing in your head? How do you handle challenges or failures? The conversation you hold with yourself will reveal how much you choose to be in a Victim mode. When I mentioned this revelation to Jeff, he smiled knowingly and said, "It always starts there first." The outer conversation is just a mirror of the inner conversation.

The Parent/Child/Victim relationship is also masked with other names like Boss/Employee/Underperformer or Teacher/Student/Underachiever.

Healthier relationships begin with a shared interest or intention with every person you communicate with. Jeff referred to this as the Co-creative relationship. Think of it as simply a person-to-person relationship. Both parties hold 100% responsibility and are in charge of the communication; all parties are equally important and everyone leaves affected in some way by the communication. The idea is that your intention is to truly help them win and help them communicate and learn from one another. Even if your title says that you are the president of the company, don't you still have something to learn from any employee in the company? Doesn't each person contribute to the purpose of the company and doesn't each person deserve the respect of the other?

I remember the first time Jeff instructed the corporate team I was on, about Co-Creative conversations. He gave us a great example about coaching an American football junior team. He said, "I like to coach youth football teams and sometimes I like to see how much this process of growth applies to kids. Well I coached this one football team and we didn't have much talent on the team, but I could see that each of the kids wanted to do their best and were looking to me as the coach to help them win." Jeff continued, "I wasn't sure we were going to win even one game, but this was our team and I wanted to make sure each child walked away feeling good about the season."

Jeff decided early on in coaching this team that he was going to employ the idea of a Co-Creative relationship. "Instead of yelling at the kids," he said, "I'd pull them aside and ask them what they could have done better. I also pulled the team into frequent huddles and posed questions to help them understand their role by asking the "what if" questions." Jeff said that each of the team members responded by coming up with their own solutions. Soon the team was working well together as good teams should. The season started and they won several of their first games.

With a wry smile, Jeff said, "I thought I'd try an experiment." I knew where he was going with this and I thought it was funny that he'd experiment at the expense of these kids' football season. "I decided to start using the Parent/Child method of working with the team. I began to yell more and more at certain players to do things. I questioned their decisions on the field and I frequently yelled out instructions to the players while they were playing, which was a big distraction. It didn't take long before the kids were confused at what they were supposed to do. They questioned their own performance and the performance of other teammates. And they pointed the finger at other players when the defense broke down and the other team made a big play or scored."

I could see myself experiencing what these young football players were going through. I have played, coached, and refereed sports teams and I've seen enough coaches to understand the feelings and emotions of these young kids in pads running up and down the field.

It was easy to guess what happened to the team. They lost a couple of games in a row and began to question themselves. They went from being winners to losers in a matter of weeks – in their minds anyway. I suppose being a coach who wants people to experience success, Jeff turned back to the Co-Creative method of communication. I'm not sure if he pointed out to the kids what he had done, but he did restore their belief that they could win and work with each other as a team.

Jeff said, "In no time, they were winning again, without any stars, just knowing their roles, investing their efforts and intention to win and all because there was an open communication that allowed them to use their minds and hearts to find solutions."

Jeff later told me, "I've tried that same experiment on other teams I've coached. And the fascinating thing about it is that some teams can use that love motivation and run with it while others you just have to hold them in fear motivation because that is the way they've been raised. They had the pattern instilled in them that if they think for themselves and make a mistake, they will be punished for it. The other part of that equation is that many of the teams that came from a higher social-economic background were trained to think for themselves, while those that came from lower social-economic classes were more fear motivated. I guess that is why money doesn't show up in a fear motivated environment – just like love motivation doesn't show up there either."

I understand the Co-Creative communication and I'd previously thought of it as a win-win relationship. But like most efforts to change ourselves, it was easy to understand, but harder to do it out of habit. Now I've had more time to contemplate this concept over the years, I think of it as a co-creative communication. Two or more people join together in a communication, no matter how small, and walk away knowing, feeling, and enjoying something that wasn't there before. This co-creative communication starts without any judgment – only an intention to explore and find shared purpose. It starts with curiosity.

Only strength can cooperate. Weakness can only beg.
– Dwight D. Eisenhower

A co-creative experience is motivated out of love and abundance. A co-creative communication or relationship is one between two or more people who are secure in their emotions and in their purpose. They trust themselves and they trust that others are there to help them with their purpose. They are responsible and own their experience. They trust that no matter the outcome, they will learn something from the experience. They look for win-win opportunities wherever they are.

This can easily be you. You can encourage instead of discourage and add to the overall communication and shared experience. As you achieve this, you see the world through abundance and want others to see the same way, but realize that not all will have the same degree of understanding and awareness. After you understand what they want and what they want is not in alignment with your purpose or that they can't provide what you need to achieve your goals, then it becomes easy to part ways. You see and choose a positive outcome and when you realize that the outcome from a particular conversation will not take you toward your purpose, you seek to win by understanding and finding ways to learn from the other person or the experience. As a "Co-Creative person" you wish the other person well or bless them in your heart and you move to the next experience to further their purpose.

A Co-Creative communication doesn't have to come from an adult at all. An example of this is how my son, who was five at the time, acted with me when we were playing around and he got hurt:

> I Still Believe In You Dad
> November 3
>
> I'm not sure what it was that I did to my youngest son, I think all the kids were wrestling around with me on the couch and he slipped off. I grabbed his leg, but that only made him fall headfirst onto the floor. He winced a little and rubbed his head. He was on the verge of crying. I apologized to him saying, "Sorry, I wish I could have caught you."
> He reached up to me and said, "That's okay, I still believe in you dad." I scooped him up in my arms and rubbed the back of his head. I buried my face in his neck and told him that I loved him. He is a special kid. I have four very special children.

I could have reacted or said something different to my youngest son like, "Come on, be tough!" He could have just as easily been a victim by crying and running off, because I knew it hurt him. Instead, he reacted in a very rational manner and helped lift me with his response. That is what a Co-Creative communication is about.

Ask Your Neighbor

Jeff told me about a youth group that he took through a training program. One of the experiences he wanted to create for these youth was the idea that people will reflect back to you what you need to know.

He met these students in a mall and gave them a sheet of paper. On the paper was a quick little script on what to say. It said:

"I am taking a life strategies class, and I would like to ask you to help me by answering some easy questions. Please take a look at me, and tell me what kind of person you think I am.

I will be taking notes while you are talking – go ahead." There was space below the script to write notes. Half way down the page was the second question, which said, "Thank you. Now, will you please share with me advice that you believe will help me in the future?"

I could imagine how much fear that little exchange would create for me, but I was interested to know what people might say about me. My opportunity to experience this came up the next time I went through the Intentional Vision with someone I was taking through as a coach. I didn't hesitate to try the experiment out for myself. The following excerpt from my journal relates to part of that experience:

> Mall Experiment
> December 2
>
> What a great time to go do my homework in the mall! I went to the mall to see if I could complete my homework with the hordes of people shopping for Christmas.

The first person I talked to was a young lady in a bookstore. I wandered around for a few minutes looking for the self-help section and she stood out with a big smile. She asked me, "Can I help you?"

I replied, "Yes you can." I took a deep breath and said, "I'm looking for a book by Deepak Chopra and I want to ask you two questions." She nodded her consent. I spread my arms out like I was opening the kimono and said, "Take a look at me and tell me something about me, about my characteristics."

I tagged another of the ladies working in the bookstore and then I went out into the hall to find a captive audience. There was a very long line of people all waiting to take their kids to see Elmo and another line to see Santa Claus. I had a fun time talking to different people and getting their thoughts and advice. I also thought it was interesting how people gave me advice about what they were experiencing in life.

One young fellow who was in his early twenties said, "Stay in school. I'm in middle management and I can't go any further without going back to school. But you need to keep learning. I know this and I'm reading a book on management every month." Then his next bit of advice was this, "Find your passion and go for it!"

He was the only fellow who I gave advice back to. I said, "Life is a mirror and the advice you're giving me is advice you need to consider in your life. However, I will tell you that you don't necessarily need a formal education to succeed. The part you said about having a passion and going for it, that is the most important advice you need to take to heart." He sincerely thanked me for the reflected advice.

I only had two problems with the homework assignment. First, we were supposed to approach different people with two different feelings – one as an indifferent stranger and the other as a friend. I couldn't approach anyone other than as a "good friend," so I only felt the energy from that direction. The other problem is – this experience tends to push a very Blue person away from their comfort zone. I believe if I hadn't taken this type of training in the past and hadn't known my purpose, I wouldn't have followed through with it. It would have scared me to death to approach so many strangers. Instead, it was a great experience to hear from other people all the nice things they had to say about me. I received lots of compliments and everyone thought I was about 7-10 years younger than I am. Score! Big win!

I realized as I went through the exercise that people were more than willing to help me and that in a way, I might have helped them too. It was also very easy to see the people who were not willing to share their thoughts with me and I wondered if they were stuck in any part of their life.

I did get rejected by one older fellow, who didn't allow me to say more than, "Hello, I'm taking a life strategies course…" To which he abruptly replied, "I don't want anything to do with that." I don't take rejection well and it's been a major part of my experience of fear in life. I slipped into a Radio Shack store for just a minute to look at their TV monitors, took a breath and let the thought come that, "I'm okay and he's okay, too." I left the Radio Shack and immediately was greeted with a "Happy Holidays" greeting by a cell phone salesman. I knew he was there for a reason and I switched gears to have him and his lovely co-worker help me with my reflective perception project. I gave each person a heartfelt compliment, and I wished them well in their well-wishing and I left knowing I'd learned and shared with others. I allowed strangers to communicate some of life's messages to me.

Here is something that might give some people a little pause to think. If you aren't willing to step outside your box and ask your neighbor for his or her help and advice, then you don't trust yourself.

Think about this, if you completely trust yourself, you will trust others too and what could they do or say about you that would really reject you? Even if they were to reject you and you trusted yourself in the experience, it would be easy to turn to the next neighbor and ask for their help.

Making It Crystal Clear

1) How do you see and interact with others? Do you interact as a parent or boss with a win/lose attitude? Do you act the part of the child with a lose/win outlook? Or do you choose to be a victim with the lose/lose mentality? How often do you play the co-creator role where you see that you're okay and they're okay and seek to be creative in your communications?

2) Co-creative conversations begin with the thought that no matter what, this conversation or interaction will be perfect and they progress with curiosity on both sides.

3) When you trust yourself, you can truly trust your neighbor – including any strangers with whom you come in contact – and you can ask your neighbor to help you and tell you things you need to know about you.

Intentional Vision Exercises

1) Review your kryptonite or major weakness (refer to the chart you created in the previous exercises) and ask yourself, "What was my kryptonite trying to teach me about myself and how I gain love and acceptance?"

2) Describe what you do to overcome being heavy in your attitude, so you can routinely become lighter in your attitude.

3) Share with one person in your life how you find emotional reward (how you pay yourself).

4) Continue to write about things that make you happy or feel in abundance.

5) Who do you still need to forgive for the pain you feel in your life?

Chapter 6

Choosing Your Rules
Your Kryptonite Is Embedded In Your Rules of Life

The limits of your language are the limits of your world."
– Ludwig Wittgenstein

We are not blank tablets when we come to this life experience. However, our parents will write plenty on our empty pages, which will affect how we look at and perceive this life experience. So does that make you a victim of your parents' programming? Absolutely not! The good news is you can rewrite the patterns or you can create new meaning for them, but you first must be aware of the patterns and stories that are the "limits of your world."

Jeff helped me to see some of the patterns in my life and recognize where they came from and why they were there. He also gave me a great insight on how to create habits and how long it really takes to make a pattern change stick. It's easy to see great results in the first 21 to 30 days with any self-development process, "But then you hit a major pothole. Nearly everyone does it. It's just your intending mind and imprinted mind testing out the new patterns you're writing in your mind. Once you understand this, then you will have a breakthrough in your progression."

If you are following the Intentional Vision program, doing the weekly reading and the homework assignments, this might be the time when self-sabotage can come up. Self-sabotage is an energy burst from your kryptonite or major weakness. When you first start a self-improvement program of any type, it takes approximately 21 days of the intending mind focusing on change to start to formulate new habits or patterns. So the old adage of "It takes 21 days to form a habit" is only partly true. The next 21 days is when the imprinted mind uses the new patterns and takes them for a test spin to see if it can still hold your innate mind in safety. When I say "test spin", there should be more emphasis on the "spin" part, because you may feel like life is spinning out of control.

Your kryptonite is locked up in your imprinted or subconscious mind. Remember, it's trying to protect you from what has hurt you in the past. Here's the good news though. Most people only have one or two sabotaging experiences, which will most likely only last a few days to a week. Just grit your teeth, know that it's something you get to learn from, and move ahead with your new habits.

Many professionals who help people change self-defeating habits, such as personal trainers, marriage councilors and motivational experts, understand that it's easy to see results in the first 21-30 days, but the next 21-30 days are crucial, because that's when your imprinted mind pushes back to really see if you want to write these new habits and patterns in your mind and body. Many professionals will commit you to a certain period of time in order to keep you from backing out of your personal commitment. For example, Harville Hendrix, Ph.D. is a leading couples therapist and best selling author. In his book, *Getting the Love You Want*, he states that one of the first rules he gives couples is that they commit to at least 12 weekly sessions with him, barring a true emergency. He then states why, "I know from my own experience, and from statistical surveys, that a majority of couples quit therapy somewhere between the third and the fifth appointments, which is about the time it takes for unconscious issues to begin to emerge and for people to begin to experience some anxiety. As we all know, a tried and true method for reducing anxiety is avoidance." This comment validates for me that this Intentional Vision process is making a difference by the way it follows the same rules of building habits and overcoming the self-sabotaging patterns.

Let me point out that if you are starting to get some negative results or feelings in life after 21-30 days, it's your mind's natural way of creating, testing and adopting change. Everything has to pass through you kryptonite filter. If you will go another 21-30 days beyond the initial three to five weeks, you will begin the process of truly owning the habit or new pattern of thinking in your life. If you don't believe this, go ask anyone who runs a fitness center how long it takes to get in shape and to get in a lifelong habit of staying in shape, and they will most likely tell you 90 days. Then ask them how many people drop out after three to six weeks. Many drop out because they don't understand what is going on in their minds and bodies. So stick with it! Do the reading and assignments and be curious about the changes you experience.

Clarity of Freedom
(Week 5 Reading Assignment)

When you choose more Responsibility, you earn more Power, and when you gain more Power, you earn more Freedom.

Examine a group or organization you know and see if the same person who has the most responsibility is also the one with the most power and ability to have the most freedom.

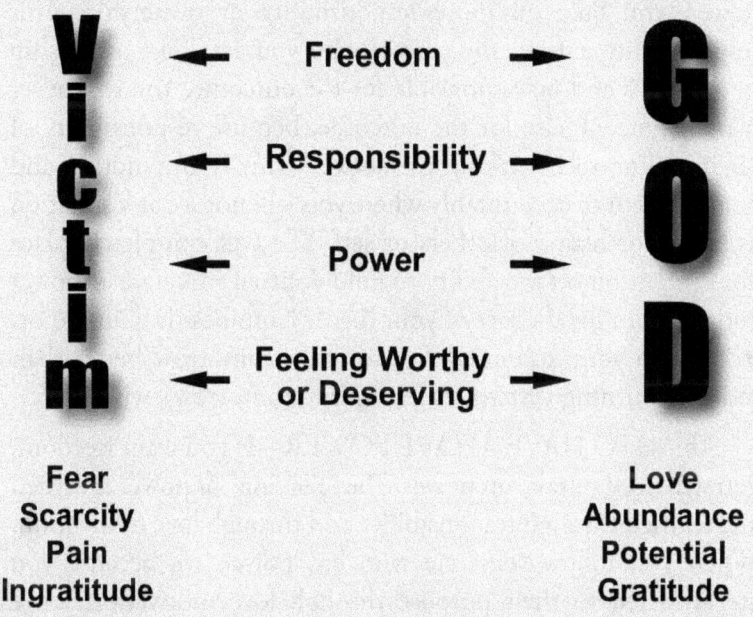

Fear
Scarcity
Pain
Ingratitude

Love
Abundance
Potential
Gratitude

Our planet fits this model, with the Creator/God having the most (on the right) and a Victim having the least (on the left). A victim doesn't feel worthy, causing him or her to not choose responsibility; therefore, he or she stays a victim due to lack of power and limited freedom.

This is a BE – DO – HAVE with PURPOSE process, and it works very fast to gain personal freedom.

First: TO BE – BE Worthy – The first step to accomplish your ultimate desire is to overcome past emotional challenges. Your life depends on it, that is the life you deserve. Let go of the past, remind yourself that you have a purpose to exchange with the Universe and any fear-based learning you've had is in preparation to learn how to experience love-based motivation.

Second: TO DO – DO it in RESPONSIBILITY/ACCOUNTABILITY/OWNERSHIP – If you want more power, you take on more responsibility or ownership. This responsibility is from the core of who you are. Take ownership in the goals and be responsible for the outcome. You can never blame someone else for the outcome, because responsibility of "If it's going to be, it's up to me/we." This is an emotion and commitment of accountably where you will not see any situation as shame or blame of others or self. You will completely place your intention on the ability to hold yourself in a state of power and freedom for the rest of your life. If happiness is going to be, it is up to your accountability to make tomorrow better than today by turning yesterday's lesson into tomorrow's wisdom.

Third: TO HAVE – HAVE POWER – If you want freedom, you will need to take on power. The "Having" of power is earned and learned through responsibility and through love motivation. When you follow someone who has power, it's because you are attracted to their purpose through love motivation. Love motivation is the emotion of co-creation or "Win–Win," and with this love motivation you will help others gain what they want by doing what is good for the team or organization. When you are doing power, you are empowering others to get what they want personally, so they are motivated to accomplish what you and your team wants and needs.

Fourth: with PURPOSE – FREEDOM – Freedom is the ability to make choices; choices based on who you are, which creates a life filled with joy and freedom. Freedom is making choices without permission, without fear, and without memories of pain; freedom to be at your greatest potential while experiencing love, gratitude, and abundance. More freedom equals more choices, and the ultimate choice is to choose what you experience as love – the ability to love and be loved.

God is the perfect example of the Be-Do-Have with Purpose process. God is in a perfect state of <u>being</u> love and in an ultimate state of accomplishing everything through power, because of love motivation. <u>God has the supreme position of having complete freedom to have the experience of creation and with this freedom comes the experience of endless love and abundance in the universe.</u>

God's success formula is also a Be-Do-Have with Purpose process. If you are in a state of Being love with self, then you will Do love with your neighbor and you will Have or experience the love of God and co-creating more love with God and the Universe.

The Role of the Subconscious or Imprinted Mind

I can't help believing that these things that come from the subconscious mind have a sort of truth to them. It may not be a scientific truth, but it's psychological truth.
– Brian Aldiss

Understanding the subconscious or imprinted mind is key to understanding the reason why you act and feel as you do. There is that age-old discussion that takes place about whether it is nature or nurture that drives you to be the way you are and act as you do. If you're stuck in the predicament of wondering whether it's how you were born or if it's your parents that made you this way, you're right on both accounts. And it was your choice to experience it this way. If you don't believe that, then you might want to reexamine whether or not you own this experience and whether your current belief empowers you or allows you to choose to be a victim more easily.

The imprinted mind or subconscious mind is the identity that stores all the rules, patterns, programs, stories, and habits that affect how you feel about your environment and the people around you. It is the safety filter and interpretive layer for the innate mind. The rules and programs you have in your imprinted mind are what drive you to accept or reject yourself and others. The imprinted mind controls that voice of judgment about yourself and others and how you experience fairness and justice.

The imprinted mind holds information like a computer hard drive. It can help focus the mind by comparing to past experiences or create random thoughts when what you're doing has nothing to compare with. Your mental blind spots are also a part of the imprinted thinking that keep you from being able to see new thoughts or ideas. The imprinted mind is what allows you to trust or not trust, opening your mind or closing your mind.

When eastern philosophies and people who delve into the metaphysical talk about Mind-Body-Spirit, the imprinted mind is mostly related to the body or the physical experience in this life. Except for lower level body functions like breathing and your heartbeat, which are controlled by the innate, the imprinted mind is what controls all the things your body has learned to do since birth. The imprinted mind is where your learned skills are stored and are retrieved when needed. It helps you do anything that can be committed to habit, such as driving the car without thinking about it. You may have heard that "repetition is the mother of all skill," well it is also the mother of the imprinted mind. This not only goes for the repetitive tasks you learn to do, but also the repetitive patterns your mother and father instill in you.

Because of the power the imprinted has over the innate mind and the power it has to trigger emotions, it is the one that can give you the most long-term benefit if it is realigned or reprogrammed to help you reach your goals and potential.

Because the imprinted or subconscious mind is the one that stores our kryptonite and all of our other patterns of thought, if we are to make changes this is the mind we need to focus on the most. It is important to see how the imprinted mind interacts with either our intending or innate mind. Here are a few examples of how the imprinted changes our perception of how we interpret the world.

- Even though all the evidence may suggest otherwise to the intending mind, we can work on our imprinted minds to believe that smoking a cigarette brings pleasure enough that it will filter or suggest to the innate that it's safe to smoke the cigarette.
- We can say to ourselves consciously, "I'm going to eat healthy foods from now on," but the imprinted mind sees that the intending mind is feeling a need and it says to the innate mind, "It's okay to eat these chocolate chip cookies, you'll feel better when you eat them and only a few won't hurt you."
- A person mentions to you (your intending mind) about a person who is retired – the intending mind will say, "I know a retired person." The imprinted mind will put in a filter and say, "The person must be old."

The major role again of the imprinted mind is to store programs or habits and to act as a filter to help the innate mind (spirit) feel safe in this experience. What happens is the imprinted mind ends up acting on its own, without conscious interaction and it maintains a set of programs or stories that tells the innate mind that it's safe or unsafe. Unless you reprogram the imprinted to see it a different way, to tell a more complete and positive story, you will always have the same results in your life, especially when you're older.

There is a phrase that defines insanity that goes something like this – "Insanity is doing the same thing over and over again and expecting different results." If that truly is insanity, then most people in the world live it on a daily basis.

Think of your emotional patterns as skills you've learned over the years. If you want new skills to gain better results with your emotions and with your life, you'll need to create and practice in order to replace the old set of emotional skills.

Whose Rules And Stories Are These Anyway?

Jeff presented me with the idea, "How do I become the best I can be?" which is an internal drive that rests within us. We can decide whether or not to heed that call and then set off on our quest through our experiences. This drive to be better than we are comes from the innate mind. How do we come to be our best? When we can unify our intending, imprinted and innate minds – peace happens – we are in the zone. You feel not only spiritually connected, but you know who you are and you can sense and see your potential. This is called the SuperConscious or being involved in the Collective Conscious with the ability to co-create with God and the Universe.

If we can connect from the intending mind to the innate mind, we can access immense potential and power. This is what meditation is. It's turning off the imprinted mind (emptying your mind and your judgments) and your kryptonite. The intending mind keeps the imprinted so busy that the innate mind becomes available and it overflows into the spiritual resources and the co-creating collective consciousness – God.

This is why driving (not in heavy traffic) can be a nice experience, because you tie up the imprinted mind with the actions of driving and new resources can be used. Have you ever experienced an epiphany while driving or doing some other process that ties up your body in imprinted movement? Mozart used to stand at a billiard table and bounce a ball off the sidewalls in a very consistent pattern as he wrote his symphonic masterpieces. He was tying up his imprinted to access his genius within the innate mind. Ingenuity comes through an almost outside experience. Again, if we can align the intending, imprinted and the innate minds, then we enter the SuperConscious experience, which is the spiritual feeling.

At this point in the conversation, I started to ask Jeff a few questions, because I wasn't sure whether everyone really is on a quest to become a better person, "If we are built with this internal desire to be our best, then why do many people strive for mediocrity? Are they just telling themselves stories from their imprinted (kryptonite) to protect their insecure innate mind?"

Jeff clarified the reason people get stuck in their own stories, "If we tell ourselves a story long enough, it will overwrite the original program. Those overwriting stories are, 'I'm not good enough – I'm not smart enough – I'm not pretty enough…' They are lower energy stories than the original high-energy story we were created with. Our minds can only believe one thing comfortably. We can't believe, for example, that we are good looking and then on the other hand we aren't good looking. It's forced to make a decision, a choice. So instead, we tell a new story that we are just mediocre. We compromise and lose that energy we had when we started. Then we overwrite the program with our new belief about ourselves by telling ourselves – especially the imprinted mind – that it's not worth the conflict or the pain to become better."

When Jeff talked about this, it made me think of people who begin their learning journey with me doing karate. Here is an example of how I experience this when I'm teaching someone who is just starting to learn karate. I usually promote my karate business with an introductory offer that gives the potential student a karate uniform and two private lessons. In the private lessons, if the potential student is a child, we invite the parents to be there to watch as they learn and witness their child's potential in becoming better. After doing several kicks at a lower height, I ask the potential student, "How high can you kick? Show me with your hand, not with your foot." My point in this is to see how high they see themselves kicking in their minds. It tells me how confident they are in themselves. Interestingly enough, most students that are in my Little Ninja group (ages 4-6) will often put their hand to the top of their head or way over their head. At this age, they haven't set limits on themselves because their subconscious minds haven't kicked in sufficiently; however, their subconscious or imprinted minds are in the process of being programmed by life to see limits on themselves.

Now if I ask the same question to someone who is between the ages of 7-12 years old, I often get the opposite. They will put their hand down closer to their chest, even if they've already been kicking that high. It never ceases to amaze me that they have already been kicking that high and now they don't think they can kick any higher. They're starting to get those self-limiting beliefs in place and beginning to think that this is the way they should be. Finally, if I ask the same question to an older teen or adult, their answers will vary based on their self-confidence. However, almost in every case, people can kick higher than they think they can the very first time they attempt it.

We are born with unlimited potential in our innate mind. It is after we've been programmed by the large people and others in our life's experience, and then had it reinforced by what we've seen or experienced, that we set our limitations and store them in our imprinted mind.

You might be thinking, "Aha! My parents are to blame for all my limitations then." If you're saying that in your mind, then ask yourself, "Why did I pick my parents?" You might even want to ask yourself, "Why did my parents pick me?" And then the other question is, "What can I, or my parents, be learning from this experience?"

In my conversation with Jeff, he followed this thought up with, "We are often told that we spend the first short period of life being raised by our parents and then we spend the rest of our lives dealing with what our parents taught us. The truth could just as easily be the reverse from that. If we are all here for a spiritual journey, then we were born to our parents when they needed to learn something. I have my child and I dump my negative programs on them. Then when they get older – like when they become teenagers – they dump that negative programming back on me. If I'm aware of it, I can see and understand my weakness and what I need to improve – it's a mirror.

I chuckled at this image of our children being mirrors for us to look in. The image of looking in a large ornate mirror flashed up in my mind and I could see myself standing in front of it and the reflection of my oldest daughter standing in the mirror. She has turned into a true teenager and I'm seeing some of those patterns already being dumped back onto my wife and me. I also saw my oldest son, standing as a reflection of me and wondering what I was learning from him. Although he isn't acting like a teenager yet, I'm starting to see the types of patterns I've given him and how he's starting to develop his intending mind.

Jeff continued, "I can't see the program running in my own head, I can only see it running in someone else. It's important to point out that if my child is doing something that is really bothering me, then it most likely is a negative program I get to work through. And to work through this means changing it in my life, so that my child has an example of how to change it in their life. Now I can grow spiritually better with my child's help and the great thing is that when they show me my bad programs, I can change the programs and help my child understand and change their programs.

In most cases, I don't need to talk to my child, because when I have the awareness and make the change, my child almost changes magically before me. That means if I'm 60 years old, I can still go back and help my 40-year-old child understand the bad program I gave him. In the process, that 40-year-old child can go back to his 20-year-old son and help him figure out the program in his life. Or this could go the other way, is the 20-year-old helping the 60-year-old or the other way around. That is how spiritual evolution takes place. It's okay to say that I'm working through my own spiritual evolution and we are given plenty of baggage that we don't need from our parents, but that's what we get to do. It's part of the journey. After all, you need to have some baggage to take on your journey." Jeff gave me a rye smile after saying that last remark. I could just imagine the extra baggage I like to take on my trips.

In reference to coming to this existence and having our minds erased or having some kind of veil drawn across our minds, Jeff said, "A way past this veil-like experience is through meditation. It is common for many people that go through meditation to have spiritual experiences all the time. I often experience Christ during my meditations. It's common for me to experience people who have passed away, like loved ones. I'm not referencing having a thought about them, I'm talking about them standing in front of me and I'm having a conversation with them."

I then had to relate a thought that came to mind about a possible second veil, one involving our imprinted mind which kicks in when we're older and we're starting to play back more and more of the patterns we received from our parents and others. In other words, it gets harder and harder to experience life like a child again.

Jeff said, "The more effective we can get rid of this imprinted programming – or rather reprogram it – then the subconscious pattern makes it easier to work with the truth in the innate mind. When the innate mind recognizes the truth again, that's when you experience safety and love. That's when our relationship with God comes back into our awareness."

At that moment I realized that, "If you clear up that second veil or imprinted, then you experience a spiritual rebirth." When individuals start working to clear up the imprinted patterns to work toward their purpose and connecting with the innate mind, they will often experience that rebirth. I said, "Then that is really were the clarity of this whole process comes." Jeff nodded his head, knowing that I was getting it and he agreed that most of the work comes in that area – just aligning the imprinted so that the intending and the innate minds can communicate more directly toward a common purpose.

So what are the results when we don't have the subconscious in the way and we're working toward our purpose? Jeff knew this person in high school, who we'll call Tony. He was born with some learning disabilities and had a significant stuttering problem, which made it hard for him to communicate. He was a big man with a big heart.

He went to shop class every day and he graduated from high school with an amazing ability to fix cars. When Tony graduated, he went to find a job. One shop owner said to Tony, "I don't need any help right now. But I'll tell you what, you see that old car, I'll give that to you, you can fix it up and you can sell it." Tony took that one car and fixed it up and sold it. Then he took the money from that and bought and fixed up other old cars. It was a simple formula. He didn't worry about the future and he didn't worry about the past, there were no inhibitions. By the time he was 40, he had made his first million.

Jeff said, "You see Tony didn't have all the stories running in his head about why he couldn't do it. People probably told him he couldn't do it, but those suggestions never stuck, because his mind was a little different. He's always focusing on results and nothing more – 'where do I buy the next car?' He's even been on the cover of a few automobile magazines. He learned early on that he could make the most money by finding the oldest cars and fixing them up. Simple, isn't it? Especially if you don't have all the conflicting stories running in your imprinted mind. He didn't have any aspirations, only to follow what felt like his purpose. Someone told him he ought to enter his cars in competitions – he did and he won national competitions.

Success, true success at every level, is all about getting into the SuperConscious. You either have to deactivate the imprinted, like Tony, or you need to reprogram it and that's what this Intentional Vision process is about."

As I listened to Jeff, I made the jump in my mind to how large businesses have processes that drive many of their business systems. Businesses will often experience success with a process and therefore it becomes a pattern that the business imprinted mind runs, without much emotion. The trick is that you want less emotion tied up with the processes and more positive emotion within the people inside the organization. In other words, get their conscious or intending minds working toward a common purpose, a common mission. However, in today's business environment, businesses have to be flexible with their processes, so that their "imprinted" processes don't put them in danger when their business environment changes. Businesses have to rewrite their imprinted minds too – or the stories their management tells themselves. It's the business leaders that not only can reprogram their personal thinking and behavior, but can also reprogram the imprinted mind of their businesses.

Rewriting The Stories

> *There is nothing good nor bad, but thinking makes it so.*
> – William Shakespeare

Jeff peaked my curiosity. I'm always digging and prying for more information because I want to understand something in great depth. I feel more confident when I know something really well. The reason I started probing for more answers is because I wanted to make sure I could rewrite my imprinted mind and not always go back to the habits and programs that give me negative or empty emotions about life. I asked Jeff, "I know there are a few different ways to rewrite your imprinted mind, but how do you do it? How do you rewrite your imprinted mind?"

Jeff said, "There are really only three ways to rewrite the imprinted programming. The quickest way is to have a near death or after death experience. People usually come away from these experiences seeing life in a whole different way with a greater sense for their most important priorities and what they want out of life. People who have lived through a near death or after death experience will often come back with a divining question, 'Is this important? Is this important? Is this important?' The question becomes so powerful that it helps erase many of the old patterns, so that they can be rewritten. In nearly every case I've read about someone coming back from an after death experience, when they come back, they say, 'Life is easy, why was I so worried? Life is so simple. I love life. Life is so loving. I love people…' The stories that are running in their heads are now narrowed down to a much simpler set of stories. I have seen this same experience, but to a lesser degree, if someone close dies, like a loved one."

I thought, "It's too bad that everyone doesn't think of life as a near death experience." It also made me think of a popular song from Tim McGraw, Live Like You Were Dying. I'm always moved by that song and how living like you were dying is making sure you enjoy every moment in this life experience. I can just hear Tim singing it with such conviction... "I went sky diving, I went rocky mountain climbing, I went 2.7 seconds on a bull named Fu Manchu. And I loved deeper, and I spoke sweeter, and I gave forgiveness I've been denyin', and someday I hope you get the chance to live like you were dyin'...'"

The interesting aspect about that song is that the voice behind the first chorus is that of a father, who after finding out he's dying, embraces life. Then after the son learns from his father to live like he were dying, he embraces life too and the following choruses are his voice saying that he followed in his father's footsteps and did the same things. However, in the last chorus, the voice of the son says that, "...I loved deeper, and I spoke sweeter, and I watched an eagle as it was flyin.'" How apropos the symbolism that his father gave him his wings, so he could fly higher. This message in the song is exactly what Jeff talked about earlier in our conversation about spiritual evolution taking place, by handing down wisdom about the negative patterns we've planted in our posterity and finding abundance in life with another set of beliefs.

Jeff continued, "But for most of us, that near death experience isn't going to happen. So what's the next best way to rewrite the imprinted mind? The best way to rewrite with a lasting effect is to do things through repetition until a new program is established and the old one fades away. We know this pattern is a good one to break old habits and establish new ones. However, this pattern isn't used as thoroughly as it could be when intentionally targeting certain outdated patterns. The closest experience that many people have to this repetitive rewriting of the imprinted mind is when people read the scriptures from their belief systems over and over again. It could be the Bible, the Sanscrit, the Torah or the Quran. Whatever it is, that becomes scripture. If you read it enough, it will rewrite your stories, rules, and programming. And soon, you will be able to gain greater knowledge through insights and connections you would never have seen before. This system (Intentional Vision) of addressing your life, business, relationships, and spirituality relies heavily on repetition, which provides the deepest results."

Jeff then stated, "All changes go through a three step process. First it takes awareness that a change is wanted. And many times because our past patterns are so dominant, it is hard to see life in any other way. This is why the process of repetition creates a deep understanding of awareness. It allows our brain to see new possibilities that it couldn't see before. The next step is to create an agreement with ourselves or someone else as to what steps need to take place. The final step is taking the action. So the three steps are awareness, agreement and action to make any changes in your life."

I had already drawn the same conclusion about the Intentional Vision process and anyone who uses affirmations to motivate themselves. I believe the reason repetition does such a good job of rewriting the stories in your imprinted mind is because you are continually advancing in your awareness – you're learning a process of how to gain further awareness. I began from this time forward to view the Intentional Vision process as a new way of scripting my life or creating my own scriptures for life along with the ones I already believe in.

As mentioned in the opening chapters of this book, if you decide to read and reread this book and follow the steps within, you will begin to rewrite many of the negative patterns and stories that are stored in your imprinted mind.

Jeff said, "The third method for rewriting the imprinted is neural-linguistic programming or a method for putting you in or catching you in a moment of emotion, when you are running different programs and then altering the experience, so that you ask yourself a new set of questions and begin the rewriting process. This is the way of interrupting your program and then giving you new information. This way is a little more unpredictable, but it has its merits. This Intentional Vision program also uses some of this neural-linguistic programming, but only as an additional resource to the repetitive life-scripting process. Hypnotherapy also fits into this category."

At this point in the discussion, I was still intrigued with why an older person has a harder time changing. Jeff's answer was, "They have been lying to themselves longer. How many times has a person, who is 50 pounds overweight, lied to themselves about losing the weight? Pretty soon the imprinted mind has set up some pretty strong stories to protect the innate mind.

When Christ said we need to, 'be as a little child,' he didn't mean we had to return to that state of innocence. In my opinion, he simply meant we need to be able to use and communicate with deep curiosity to the innate or spiritual mind – the mind or personality you came to this earthly existence with. Curiosity is what removes the fear from the experience. When you're living in the passion of curiosity, you're living your life through love motivation. One of your strongest desires is to trust and align with the innate mind. Sometimes it takes a little more effort to reach the state of curiosity for some; however, it's all about the desire. The yearning and desire to find your purpose and change overrides any age barrier."

The Intentional Vision process has brought me closer to a state of a child than any other process I've been through. My curiosity is constantly looking for new connections and answers to deeper questions about me, my existence, and my purpose in this life experience.

Judgment Day

Here's how I experienced the way certain rules have been governing my thinking and actions. "When you are judging, you can't feel justice." When Jeff first said that to me, I thought I knew what he meant, but I really didn't get it. I didn't get it until I realized that every day is judgment day as long as I hold myself in judgment.

I asked Jeff, "Could you repeat that, I want to make sure I got it." He repeated it back to me just a little differently.

"You can't feel justice, when you're in a state of judgment." I felt like I got the gist of the statement, but again, I wasn't at the right state of awareness. I didn't get it, but I trusted that I'd understand it more deeply. I'd just have to let my mind work on the concept for a while.

Judge not, lest ye be judged
– Jesus Christ

"Judge not, lest ye be judged" is a pretty simple statement, which carries with it such significant depth. I think it took me about six months to understand what was meant by "be judged." And since that time, it has been a daily endeavor to maintain the ability to not judge others. I believe it was in Jeff's wisdom to let me discover the meaning by myself, because by my own discovery, I could really own the concept in my life.

I actually know when the concept took hold in my mind. It was June 12. I was in a church meeting and listening to a very good lesson by a fellow who is a psychology professor. The lesson was on the signs of the times. At a certain point during the lesson, another very educated scientist raised his hand and said, "May I make a statement?"

Knowing that this individual often brings up opposing points of view, the instructor said, "I hope your comment will be a peaceful one."

And then this individual began to refute several of the ideas that we share among our church about the signs of the times. I remember certain defensive emotions rising up inside me and I felt he was driving away the spirit of the meeting. Here is what I wrote in my journal about my feelings and my discovery:

> Lesson On The Signs
> June 12
>
> I thought a little bit about what he was saying and I also caught one of his thoughts about that we are judging the signs around us with our own (misled) beliefs. At one point I felt like he was saying that we all experience truth in a different way and in another way he was saying that we need to come back to reality. So I wanted to ask, "whose reality?" And when he talked about our perception

being misguided, I wondered if this wasn't one of those who's right – we're both right – times.

The instructor handled his comments nicely, but still had a little bit of a feeling of firing back at our friendly scientist (that's how I perceived it anyway). It was then that I thought about that principle of – judge not or you will never feel justice. I also thought about some of the lessons I've learned from Jeff Allen and from my studies about the power of intention. When we are in a state of judgment, we distance ourselves from our Creator and from a feeling of abundance. And yet when we argue, isn't that a setup for judgment. Don't we look down on the other person and make radical judgments about him or her? So unless it's a discussion where the intention is to both learn something from each other, then most arguments are set up to judge one another and compete to see who is the smartest and who is the strongest. Arguments are full of judging behavior and when everything is said and done, it's hard to walk away from an argument and feel love or abundance.

Here is my definition of judgment day – it's every day we judge others or ourselves. Life is like a mirror. With the same judgment that I condemn others, I condemn myself. The subconscious or imprinted mind that keeps running those patterns, which brings up judgments, is the same mind that is talking to myself constantly about whether or not I'm doing well or that I love myself or dislike myself. It's the same voice! When I finally got this, I looked around and felt complete humility, because I realized how badly I beat myself up. And I immediately felt sympathy for anyone who was judging others. When you realize this, it makes it easier to truly love and sympathize with your so-called "enemies." What a burden to carry, to be constantly judging yourself in such a way that you feel the need to judge others.

When you are judging someone, it comes mostly from fear. Who or what do we judge most? The things and people we understand the least. If you begin to understand a person or a cause more, don't you have more empathy? Don't you start to understand, and with that new understanding, don't you stop judging so harshly. Hence the word, prejudice: to pre-judge something or someone. I now have a whole knew feeling of empathy for those who have strong prejudices, because they are judging themselves just as harshly.

In the reference from Christ about "Judge not, lest ye be judged," the "Be" in "be judged" is no different than the "Be" in the Be-Do-Have with Purpose principle, but moving in a negative or fear-driven way. If you judge yourself harshly, or BE judged, then you DO the same to others, and you HAVE the results of not experiencing justice, peace or love in your life.

I've heard it said that even a single negative thought has an impact on people. And from what I've experienced, it has an impact on at least two people – the one who thought it and the one to whom the thought was directed. However, I believe the negative thought mostly impacts the one from whose mind it originated.

Now some might say that they have to judge between one thing and another. I prefer to use the word "choose" in that case. The judgment that I'm talking about is negative judgment or placing your agency and freedom above someone else's agency and freedom.

When it comes to relationships, we have more opportunities to judge and we have more opportunities to just let go and love. It's no wonder that people who are stuck in their relationships can't move forward in other parts of their lives. This is true for nearly everyone, except the predominantly Red person. The way we feel in our Innate mind or unconscious self affects every other interaction we have with others and that we have in life.

If you judge people, you have no time to love them.
— Mother Teresa

I get the opportunity to teach students of all ages. I have seen more than a few students who have been "difficult students." Many parents will bring their kids in to karate to see if we can teach them more discipline. We have a few who have been diagnosed with Attention Deficit Disorder (ADD) too. Sometimes it makes for an interesting kind of chemistry in the classroom. However, since I've become more aware of the way I judge people, I've been able to see how judging or not judging works in the classroom. There are some kids who plain and simply defy authority. The more you push them, the more they push back.

When I've made a conscious effort to see the so called "difficult students" as someone more, they change right before my eyes. It's simply a choice. Sometimes I often have to close my eyes and imagine the student happy and doing what they need to in order to improve. It doesn't take more than a moment to change my attitude toward the student and then miracles happen. I don't think this is any different than how you look at a co-worker or a customer or a leader in your business or government. The results of your experience change as you change your judgments toward others:

> Truly Incredible Day
> March 11
> ...One of the funniest wins was what I did the other day with my Little Ninja class. I couldn't believe the amount of pent up energy that was in the class and I had three students that seemed to want to go crazy. When I asked, "Who's going to be loudest, this group here or this one over here?" They all started to ki'ai in chaos. I couldn't really tell them anything or even to stop, they just wanted to yell.
> I could feel the frustration and anxiety building rapidly inside and I decided pretty quickly that I

was going to let the whole thing pass. I sat down on the floor, placed my one hand in the other in a meditative position, closed my eyes and began to think of the students as being quiet. My Little Ninjas continued to yell, trying to disturb my meditation. I smiled.

I could hear some of the parents whispering loudly to their unruly children, "You be quiet or I'm going to pull you out of there!" I continued to smile.

Soon the voices quieted and I opened my eyes. I asked, "Are you ready to start?" The three kids that started all the ruckus started ki'aing again. I closed my eyes and continued to smile. I felt at peace with the idea that the kids could ki'ai and make noise for the entire 45 minutes and I'd just sit there, enjoying visions of kids being quiet. Soon it happened, there was silence. I opened my eyes and said in a hushed voice, "Oh, you're quiet, just how I saw you." I stood up and started the class.

When I related this win to Jeff he couldn't stop laughing. "I can just see a picture of an old, bald Chinese man sitting on the floor and saying the same thing to young pupils around him. 'Oh, you're quiet, just how I saw you.'" Jeff said he'd have to use that story somehow, somewhere.

Now how often do you think about people? All the time, right? How often do you think to yourself, "What a jerk!" or "How stupid can he be?" or "Were you raised in a barn?" or "She thinks the world of herself, doesn't she?" or "Get out of my way, I'm in a hurry" or "It's all about you, isn't it?" or "She's the teacher's pet" or "He's stuck on himself" or "Is he an idiot?"... the list goes on and on, doesn't it? How many labels and references do we have for people who don't quite fit with our expectations? You could pick just one activity in life and find a whole magnitude of expressions that define our judgments about others. Think about driving for instance. What kind of things do we think or say as we travel down the roads and highways? We even have certain hand gestures that speak volumes about our judgments.

When I went back through my journal, I constantly noticed all the judgments I made about others. How we see others is how we see ourselves and how we judge others is how we judge ourselves. Life is a mirror, which you should look in often to see your true self and your amazing potential. How you see yourself in the mirror, is how you'll see others. The wicked queen of the Disney movie *Snow White and the Seven Dwarfs*, looked in the magic mirror to affirm her beauty. If she had been focused on bringing beauty to her soul, she would have been just as beautiful as Snow White. Instead, the magic mirror told her (as if it were her imprinted mind) that she wasn't the most beautiful woman in the kingdom. Her actions toward Snow White reflected how she felt about herself and would lead to her death, because that is what she desired for Snow White.

Next time you look in the magic mirror, what will it tell you about yourself? Will there be words of love or words of judgment? Remember what Jeff told me, "You can't feel justice, when you're in a state of judgment." For that matter, you also can't feel love if you're in a state of judgment. If you want a way to inoculate or immunize yourself against the ills of judgment, then put gratitude in your experience; gratitude for your life, your family, the people who are a part of your journey, and the beauty of your world. And most importantly, have gratitude for yourself.

Jeff had me say two affirmations that really helped me stop judging my imperfections, my past failures, and myself. The first was, "I love myself by forgiving myself of past negative learning." The following week, he had me then amend this to, "I love myself and I forgive myself for past negative learning by changing _____." I put in the words, "I love myself and I forgive myself for past negative learning by changing my everyday attitudes, visions, commitments, and actions." I would further develop this same affirmation to say, "I love myself and I forgive myself for past negative learning by affirming my positive attitudes, visions, commitments and actions." I don't think

I could have reached the last version had I not felt like I'd already changed many of my thoughts and behaviors.

Another affirmation Jeff gave me to help me not judge myself so harshly was, "I love the me I created." Again, being a "Blue" person I had to add my own twist, I said, "I love the me I created, I love the me God created, and I love the me God and I are creating." Both of these affirmations offer a different voice to choose when judgments come up in my imprinted mind. I often used these affirmations when I was exercising or doing run-of-the-mill activities at home.

It is so easy to judge. It's actually a habit to judge in nearly every area of our lives. But nowhere is it more prevalent than in our home environments or with our family members. However, you can overcome those judgments. It first starts with the idea that if you have a plan and a purpose with God and that this life experience is to help you learn along your spiritual journey, then the same is true for everyone around you. Just thinking that the other person is in their experience and that they are safe in that experience makes it easy to let them be who they are. There is no need to feel threatened by their opinions or behaviors. They are who they are and they are on a spiritual quest, just like you and me.

It's also necessary to step outside yourself and become the observer. Remove the ego and just enjoy that person and their perspective. If you do this, you will feel a whole different type of love and your experience will completely change. If you change how you see another person and not judge them as anything less than yourself, you will be at peace and be able to co-create a great experience with the other person.

Once the judgment idea takes hold in your awareness, it's hard not to notice how much judging is going on around you. It's everywhere, to the point of making you numb to it. You could even say that judging is simply a way that we're taught to deal with new people and experiences in our lives.

Making It Crystal Clear

    1) The role of the subconscious mind is to store your patterns

of thought that become your habits and judgments – this is where your kryptonite or major weakness is housed.

2) Your parents or the people who raised you are the ones who helped you learned many of these patterns of thought.

Intentional Vision Exercises

1) On a new 3x5 card or sticky note, write "I am changing" and "I am letting go of the pain from past experiences and hold no fear by trusting 'the now'. I trust 'the now' by changing the way I experience ___(insert items from your lists in exercises #3 or #4)_____". This will be said at any time, when your awareness identifies that "Based on results" you are not on purpose. Continue to repeat, "I love the me I created." You will attach more to your emotions and purpose if you say these statements to yourself in the mirror. But you must feel it, it can't be said in a rote way.

2) Read your rock story out loud by replacing the word "rock"with your first name. If this experience helps enlighten you about yourself, have someone close to you write their rock story and have them read it out loud to you by replacing the word "rock" with their first name. Then share your story with them in the same way.

3) Write in your success journal what are the two or three most important things you require in a relationship.

4) Describe what it feels like to feel powerful and free.

Chapter 7

Seeing With Superhero Vision

What-You-See-Is-What-You-Get

Optical Illusions or Illusions of the Mind

Jeff told me about an interesting visual phenomenon he labeled as a scotoma or blind spot. He said that when some of the earliest explorers came to the new world, there were many of the natives who couldn't see the big ships off the shores. They only recognized that people where entering their world when they came ashore on their small boats. They had never been trained to believe that anything like a big ship existed, so their minds would not recognize what their eyes were seeing. It wasn't until the shaman pointed out the ships offshore and verbally told them to see the ships, that their minds were opened to see them. Since hearing this story, I looked up various references to validate the truth of it. There were people refuting the account while others substantiated it. It was then that I realized that it didn't matter much for me because it was my WISIWIG experience and I believe that it's possible, therefore, what I see is what I get. And those who don't believe the account, they get a WYSIWYG experience too. Maybe your ship is coming in, and all you see is a cloudy sky. Look a little closer and trust yourself to see your truth.

In a smaller way, we can explore this phenomenon of the mind filling in information that isn't physically seen. I've always been fascinated by sight and how the mind interprets it. I remember my dad showing me different optical illusions and when he pointed out that we all have blind spots, I thought that was crazy. I went home after Jeff told me about the Native Americans not seeing the ships and researched different optical illusions. I remember finding information on the Internet that showed that not only do we have a blind spot, but our minds will fill in the color from it's surrounding area in order to create a more intact picture of the world. That means that if there is a black dot in an area of green, when the black dot is in our blind spot, our mind fills in the blind spot with green. The same is true if the dot is in an area of any other color.

So in the case of a person with a Green personality, they would have a blind spot that they would fill in their experience with their green thinking style to make their experience feel whole. In other words, they project their beliefs out on others and out into the universe so they can understand it better. The miracle is that because we have different personalities, we have a world that functions better and we have people who can see our blind spots and help us out – in other words – our neighbor.

Having blind spots in your writing is very common too. It is very difficult to edit you own words, because you become so attached to the meanings you have written in your mind that you look past the typos and grammatical mistakes. You can read a sentence multiple times with a typo and not recognize it, until someone else with "fresh eyes" looks at what you've written and points it out to you. In fact, I'm sure there are still errors in this book and it will be the Green and Teal people who will find them first. Interestingly enough, Jeff used to intentionally leave errors in his course materials just to see who would point them out first. He would then use the class discussion about focusing on errors or mistakes as another proof point to how easy it is for Green and Teal to see all the things that are not perfect around them.

So our minds are eager to fill in the details when we don't have enough information. The question is what will our minds use to fill in the details. In our lives, if the picture isn't clear enough in our minds and also in our hearts, then we tend to fill in the rest with doubts or fears, unless we've trained ourselves to fill it in with trust and intention.

I believe it is possible to look off the shore and not see the ships. I know I've often gone into a room looking for something and couldn't find it, regardless of how hard I looked. And then someone picks the missing article up, which was right in front of me, as big as a ship sitting off the shore, and says, "If it had been a snake, it would have bit you."

You may want to ask if we choose not to see? The Bible and other ancient scriptures have literally hundreds of stories that demonstrate how people were either blessed or punished because they chose to see or not to see through faith and intention. So choose wisely, because you either increase love, agency and intention through what you see, or you decrease it.

Our doubts are traitors and make us lose
the good we oft might win by fearing to attempt.
– William Shakespeare

The 4th Law of Intentional Vision –
Be a Superhero… Be a Leader
(Week 6 Reading Assignment)

*"When the effective leader is finished with his work,
the people say it happened naturally."*
– Lao Tse

By taking ownership in trusting your experience (trusting Universe, trusting self, trusting others), you become a leader. As people attempt to lead others, they fall into different categories based on whether they use fear motivation, incentive motivation or love motivation. Based on the way they amplify love, we could call them: a Minimizer, Neutralizer or a Magnifier.

The Minimizer is someone no one wants on his or her team. This person is motivated by fear and doesn't exemplify trust in many areas of their life. He or she takes credit when it is positive and he or she is a finger pointer when it comes to any blame or negative results. No one trusts the Minimizer, because he or she doesn't trust himself or herself and acts irrationally or inappropriately. The Minimizer will often use their authority or title rather than any personal power or trust. Those who are managed by a Minimizer don't know how to please them. Those who work with a Minimizer are always on guard and protective. And those who manage a Minimizer would like to fire them, if given the opportunity, or at least ignore them as much as possible. Leadership that uses fear motivation has a diminishing return affect, eventually requiring more energy put in than any beneficial gain from the results (and many times there is no result at all).

The Neutralizer is someone who only gives what he or she gets. This person is motivated by incentives or rewards. The Neutralizer only trusts what he or she can see or perceive. The Neutralizer is accountable for what is required of him or her, but doesn't take full responsibility for all that happens within his or her domain. The Neutralizer is impersonal or very business-like to work with or under. He or she rarely shows emotions because he or she doesn't trust that others will understand their emotions and therefore doesn't pursue their goals with enthusiasm to fulfill his or her fullest potential. The Neutralizer rarely draws people to their cause or purpose, unless they offer a reward. Leadership that uses reward or incentive motivation as the only method of motivation has a minimal sustaining return that often reverts back to fear motivation. Neutralizers commonly motivate for their own personal gain and that's why it's not a very sustainable motivation model.

The Magnifier possesses great personal power. This person is motivated by love and truly trusts himself or herself. He or she is a "total person" that others look up to and want to emulate and be around. Everyone trusts the Magnifier and wants him or her to be on their team. The Magnifier brings more to the team or organization than he or she is compensated for. Leadership that focuses on love motivation is expansive and growing; 100% effort is given with everything being put on the line every time. Through love motivation, the Magnifier helps co-create greater solutions and a more creative environment. It's easy to spot a Magnifier, they are the ones who continually create success in their lives and in the lives of others.

This love for the challenge is what makes the champions of the world so great. For example, take any world class athlete and the countless hours he or she puts into training and practicing. Often that person won't be recognized for his or her hard work until their hard work turns into results or wins. As he or she piles up more victories their influence and popularity grows, but the hoards of endorsements and followers are in relation to how committed he or she is to loving life and serving his or her purpose.

A leader who is a Magnifier is truly a self-agent and he or she knows beyond any shadow of a doubt that, "The greatest key to success is found by looking in the mirror."

There are three levels of leadership or three basic ways a love-motivated leader magnifies everything he or she touches, by being:

1) A self leader – if you can't lead yourself, no one will follow you

2) A great follower – leading by example. A leader who feels comfortable following and knows when to do it. (It doesn't matter if you are pushing or pulling, only that you are energetically helping the team)

3) A leader of others – someone who is willing to lead others and volunteers often without thinking about it – being able to step up anytime

Notice that each of these levels of leadership correlates to the levels of consciousness. Being a self leader is about tapping into your Innate or unconscious mind. Being a greater follower is about using your socialized experiences in your Imprinted or subconscious mind. Being a leader of others is about using your Intending or conscious mind to create a greater vision and purpose to lead others. When you use the strengths of your personality, you become a greater leader with your own leadership style.

Ask yourself this question? "If I can't lead myself, who can I lead?" If you can't get out of bed on time, or can't pay your bills on time, or simply can't get up off the couch and do something with purpose, then how will you ever be able to lead others?

This does not mean you need a bigger stick to beat yourself up, but it does mean you need to take an accountable position of, "If not me, then who?" and, "If not now, then when?"

Remember the power of leadership is 'in the now', and 'Now' is a learned response. 'Later' is also a learned response, but if you are going to be successful tomorrow, it requires action today. Leadership is a learned response that starts now with self.

A leader creates a constant vision of seeing opportunities. He or she sees people as individuals who want to be their best and capable of living up to their potential. Leaders look for the things in life they are thankful for. They always see life as having an abundance of opportunities and remain open to new possibilities. They become so excited about new opportunities that the gap between seeing a goal and acting on it happens so fast that very little or no time passes.

Those who do not want to be leaders are always expressing anger, frustration, and disappointment. They have become a victim to the circumstances (which they created), placing blame for their failure on something… anything. Victims find it very hard to overcome their thought processes, because they won't choose or accept ownership for their lives; they blame the weather, the government, or even God for their life being in ruin. Remember, however, that you are the one who creates instances of sabotage and no one else.

For you to be a true leader you must possess all three levels of leadership and be a Magnifier, because sometimes you lead, sometimes you follow, and you are always a self-agent (a leader of yourself).

The underlying emotion that will hold a leader rock solid and purpose driven is to simply have a genuine trust and love for self. Now I'm not talking about blind trust or romantic love, nor is it about conceit or self-righteousness. The type of trust and love that I'm talking about is what gives you strength when the chips are down. It is the kind of trust and love where you don't lose self-respect when you have made a mistake; your self-confidence is unshakable. Without this level of trust and love for yourself, your world will remain on a shaky foundation.

The greatest tool you could ever use to maintain your God-given strengths and prevent yourself from being a victim is to trust and love yourself. Hold yourself in a higher level of pure potential, while living in gratitude and abundance.

Remember if you don't choose for yourself, someone else

will choose for you. The choice is yours to make; it is all about self-agency/self-leadership. Your innate energy came with inner strength to work through any solution without falling into the emotion of being a victim or feeling like a loser – being "stuck".

When a choice is not allowed or not promoted, then love is not honored. Love motivation requires choice, and when choice is not offered or is limited by judgment, then incentive or fear is the motivation.

As a self-agent you are in a position to always be creating, furthermore, the best way to find or feel love is to create. While creating, always look to create relationships that are co-creating, breeding success, and ultimately creating love.

To be a breeder of success you will motivate others to succeed by looking for ways to help others create for themselves, and in turn, they will be eager to help you create your vision, hence the idea of "Co-Creating."

It is an amazing experience to be in the state of co-creating a vision, your vision. You will experience higher levels of self-gratifying love than any other experience. You will also remain in a state of perpetual gratitude for what you've co-created.

To experience love one must be in the state of creating something. The human spirit will only feel the liberating emotion of love when in a state of creating, making something or someone better. When you are creating something, you lose track of time and space. You forget your hunger or need to go to the bathroom.

A good example of creating is when you are in the act of procreating or physical intimacy, you simply get lost in an emotion of bliss. Well the same is true when you are in the state of creating your vision, you will experience bliss. However, love in a relationship can be misunderstood, if you love someone to achieve self gratification then your expectations of your lover are unachievable. They don't have the ability to make you love yourself. There might be moments of great joy but in the long run it is up to you to experience love. And it is also up to you to co-create so that the other person is also winning. Feelings of love include attraction, curiosity, and the desire to nurture something to make it more than it is. Fear, however, is defensive, stagnate, and avoiding pain or losing something, which removes the desire to connect with or help other people.

Now a leader will always keep their purpose in mind. And the better a leader keeps their word with them self, the better they will keep on the path to their purpose.

I assure you that if you do not keep your word with yourself by honoring yourself, then you will start conforming to other's needs. And when you start conforming to other's needs, you will start withholding information from others, which leads to the destruction of the human spirit… your spirit. The decay of your spirit ends up in self-anger, being stuck in life and not able to act. If you react harshly to any situation, examine if it really isn't self-anger that's being manifested in your experience.

To love, trust, and respect yourself, you must keep your word with yourself (honor and trust yourself), so you will not conform to others in an unhealthy way, so you will not withhold information, causing you to feel that your point of view has no value, which would eventually turn you into a victim.

Loving, trusting and respecting yourself is the golden ticket, the magic ring, the ultimate secret to maintaining leadership!

Often people think a lifelong vacation is the best way to create a feeling of joy and happiness. In reality, how long of a vacation can one really take? One week, one month, maybe one year… and then the boredom will hit you. The food no longer is exciting, neither are the new vistas or sandy beaches, and the hotel room becomes a prison, trapping you into another night of boredom.

You have seen the Hollywood stars that self-destruct into total embarrassment. They simply thought they had arrived in bliss, stopped setting goals, went on vacation, and called it life. Eventually the self-destruction started. They no longer had a dream, they stopped keeping their word with self, then they started conforming to other's expectations of them, which led them to withholding their inner feelings… and then they end up on the cover of some magazine or on some TV show for some ridiculous act of stupidity. And soon their lives are plagued with more paparazzi following them around looking for anything else they can find to increase the amount of negativity in the star's life.

A leader is a self-agent who is in a constant state of co-creating his or her vision to serve their purpose in life. When you are creating, an inner love will grow to an unstoppable courage. This is undoubtedly the ultimate secret and satisfaction to true leadership. This ultimate leader is the one that knows how to lead themselves with love, lead others with love, and be a co-creator who teaches others how to be self agents.

When you are having a feeling of curiosity and passion build up in you, one that sets and starts the goal in the same moment, you are feeling the passion of love. It can grow and energize you so strongly that you cannot stop yourself. You simply can't ignore it; you are really feeling the desire to create.

It is that same feeling that might have gotten you in trouble as a child, the same feeling that put you on top of the dining room table doing a dance before you even thought about it. It is raw and real, and when used with wisdom this powerful feeling can move mountains, it can change the future, your future. And the ultimate feeling of power is when others are motivated at the same level to accomplish your shared goal, or in other words co-creating.

A true leader is truly love motivated and that gives them a power that others want to follow. Everyone will devote all that is possible to help a powerful person. On the other hand, a leader that is not love motivated will use authority to govern people.

And the difference between power and authority is having a choice or being forced.

This is not to say that there are times that managing others might require the use of authority because some people only understand and react to fear. And in this case one needs to use reward motivation to teach love motivation.

Many times leaders are so busy trying to force specific results that those being led cannot understand what is wanted of them. And when the leader starts teaching the reason why the results need to be done in a certain way, the others will understand quite quickly.

For example; a young child is told to go clean their room and later the room is still not clean. The parent could use authority and make the child clean the room, or the parent could offer a reward for a clean room. Now the real opportunity is to teach the child the personal value of a clean room.

I know some think that this is wrong to reward a child to clean their room, but in reality it is the only way to teach trust, which is the foundation of love. And by the way, would you do a good job at work if you were not paid – or rewarded. Leaders that can teach the why of a specific result and how it satisfies the ultimate goal will be an unstoppable leader.

Leadership that uses fear motivation has a diminishing return effect, eventually requiring more energy put in than any beneficial gain from the results (and many times there is no result at all).

Leadership that uses reward or incentive motivation has a sustaining return that is always working on trade or exchange. Producing what is necessary is the standard and will usually maintain a status quo.

Leadership that focuses on love motivation is expansive and growing; 100% effort is given with everything being put on the line every time. This is what makes the champions of the world so great.

Most people that are working on leadership qualities become stagnated because they seem to work on everything in their life except for themselves – their inner self. A leader has the trust of God and the Universe, trust of themselves, and the wisdom to know how to trust others. They also know how to lead with love, the kind of love that turns into power, the one that is always curious, expansive and growing.

A leader has a high level of curiosity and passion to be the best possible, the passion to bring out the best in the team and hold the team accountable to love. A successful leader motivates others with love and is teaching them to be a self-agent by helping them make choices and feel worthy.

When the leader teaches how to make choices, the individual will take on more responsibility, more power, and more freedom.

Don't get me wrong, you don't have to be a slow motion, over sensitive type of person to be a leader. Anybody that is playing the game with intensity to win and I mean really do whatever possible to succeed can be a leader. The kind of person that says put me in the game because I want to win with gusto and grace.

One of the fastest ways to grow your inner love is to ask someone to help you. While someone is helping you, or after the task is complete, thank and compliment him or her from the bottom of your heart, with deep meaning and energy. If you give them the compliment in the moment that they are helping you, the energy of your gratitude jumps a thousand fold for both you and the person who you are complimenting. Your compliment is telling them absolute truths about them; tell them how smart, kind or wonderful they are. Do it with real passion.

You will see the person not only gains great respect for you, but you gain a great level of self-love, self-respect, and self-trust. Your level of worthiness jumps to a new height. Most people that are working on leadership qualities become stagnated, because they seem to work on everything in their life except for themselves – their inner self.

Leaders are those who bring additional energy or synergy to any organization. They are the spirit of the organization. And everyone within the organization can be a leader in his or her own way, if they first become a self-agent.

To maintain leadership one needs to co-create and share, teach, love and be loved. And if you think you are too masculine or strong to be loved, then you will always fall short of your potential. To not be loved is one of the most selfish attitudes you can take and you will not be able to share, give, help or teach anything really meaningful in life.

Start this process by writing "I love myself and play to win by co-creating" on your mirror largely so it is easy to read. Then with sincere intent and looking closely and deeply in your eyes in a mirror repeat often (I love myself and play to win by co-creating). I know this seems silly, but if you can't do this, it is almost impossible to have an honest to goodness love for self.

It is important to understand that your list of people you want to include on your team also have their dreams, so as you ask them to be a part of your team, start the conversation that you have a dream, but you want to hear their dream first, so you can help them get it.

If you can't think on the spot to correlate how helping them will also help you and visa versa then think about it for a day or two. Sometimes the dreams that make them happy are not close enough to yours to be able to co-create. But my guess is there is almost always a way where you join talents and become a dominant force.

Be a leader that is a self agent using self love as an anchor to overcome any challenges. Then be a breeder of success, help others that are on your team to succeed at what they want and they will help you succeed at what you want.

Remember when your team member is doing the task requested, pay them a compliment and give one that is very real to you and to them, so you both can feel the love to the vital core.

So…do your Intentional Vision activities and become the leader of your own life and happiness.

Choosing To See It The Hard Way

As a kid, I used to dream of being a superhero. I had all sorts of powers I'd developed and discovered like being able to fly, shooting beams of energy from my hands and creating force fields to protect the people I was saving and myself. As I look back on the emotions or reasons I wanted to be a superhero, I find that it was the emotions of freedom, helping people, and being recognized for special talents that drove my superhero desires. I may never in this lifetime be able to fly like Superman, but I can gain many of the same emotions that I craved as a child when I dreamed of being a superhero.

I took a leap of faith and my wife had to have faith in me that we could fly when I took on my dream. However, leaving my corporate job and striking out on my own has not been the easiest experience for my wife.

Like any relationship, ours has ups and downs. I think it's only a matter of how high or low they go and for how long they last. When I left my job in the high tech field, it was with the desire to write more. For the first year, I had regular writing projects mostly from my former employer. But I hadn't written on a project to bring in money for nearly six months. I had called on a few people at my old high tech firm and I had some good leads. In fact, one fellow was about to give me a project writing a networking article for the company magazine. I don't know why, but I just couldn't pull myself in that direction. I never followed up to get the project. I felt almost repulsed by the thought of writing about something that wasn't in my heart. I've written so many things that were technical, instructional or marketing related, but I just couldn't do it this time. Looking back, I had another path in front of me and I was at a crossroads. I think my wife picked up on this feeling too. I wrote the following about what she said when I started talking to Jeff about doing this book project:

> Talking Futures
> September 29
>
> I didn't have a chance last night to talk to my wife about my conversation with Jeff Allen. I told

her that it was good news, but that was about all. It wasn't until this afternoon, when we had lunch, that I could talk to her at length. As I told her about the conversation and how it was exciting that I might just be able to do some life strategies training and do some writing on a motivational book, she told me, "The other day I had an epiphany about you. I always thought that any kind of writing would be good for you to make money. Now I realize that you need to write on something you want to write." It's funny how clear some things become once you think about it enough. It's also a little strange how everything kind of falls into place when it's the right time. I think it's the right time for this.

My wife is right, I do need to find something I can sink my teeth into, something I like to do. I'm already doing something I like to do (teaching karate), but it doesn't complete me. Now it's time to take things into my own hands and make it happen. My wife was very excited about our conversation. In fact, she told me that I had to call my sister in order to find out if I can stay at her place near Boise. That's just another thing that's kind of wild. Why is it that Jeff lives in Boise and now my sister is moving up there? Is it just another part of the puzzle, if indeed I'm going to spend a little more time in Boise?

It wasn't but a few weeks later that my wife and I had a heart-to-heart discussion. I had just started my coaching sessions with Jeff and I think my wife was reacting to some of the changes I was going through. Her emotions were closer to the surface than usual and so were mine. Here is a small portion of what we discussed:

Discussion With My Wife
November 23

I don't know how it all started, but I had a really good talk with my wife this afternoon. It was one of those heart-to-heart talks that leaves you with a few tears. Now that I think about it, I think my wife sat down to read parts of my personal identity report that talks about my personality and the way I handle things. She pointed out a few of my "flaws," while I just mentioned that they were merely traits. As my wife read on, she also read about the other color categories and quickly identified with the Red and Green sides of the quadrant. She is nearly a polar opposite of me. That's why we could be seen as being complimentary to each other.

At one point in the conversation, we talked about my vision of the karate studio. I mentioned I didn't have a real clear picture and that is probably why it's plateaued a bit. I also said that one of the reasons I felt I had an unclear vision was because she was only "tolerating" the business and not really supporting it. To me tolerating means that she allows it to continue, but there isn't any positive energy or emotion when it comes to the matter. She agreed. I even went as far as to say that in many ways, I plateaued in my business about the time she was mentally and physically checking out of the karate studio (due to our agreement that we'd hire someone to run the office after two years). I'm not sure how true it is, but I think there is some truth to the matter.

I told my wife, "I love you and I want you to find a purpose in life... I want my wife to become fulfilled." She mentioned how painful it is to deal with all the money issues on a day-to-day basis. I asked her, "If all the money problems went away, would you be happy?" Then I told her that I thought it would only take away some of the pain, but that it wouldn't really make her feel fulfilled.

One thing that I would soon learn from my wife is that I couldn't change her nor should I even attempt to, but my passion for my changes made me want to help others and I felt I needed to help my wife "see the light". What was I thinking? Jeff told me more than once that my responsibility was to "Love my wife through it." I somehow didn't trust that she would figure things out and I had to be there to help her. I needed to be a little more trusting of God, her, and myself. We were and still are in this thing together and loving her through life is the only thing I need to do. When I let go of the concept of changing her, that's when we both changed. But I was hardheaded and it took me a little while to get this, meanwhile I was still learning my lessons from my relationship with my wife.

Sex Isn't the Issue

The more and more emotions keep surfacing, the more important it is to look to see what it is teaching you. I think it may have been part of the plan or part of the growing experience for me. For example, although issues with sex can be a problem in many relationships, these issues really are only indicators of deeper emotional issues. Sex is in many ways a barometer for the emotional weather in your relationship. Jeff restated the same idea to me, "Most sexual problems are just another expression from which deeper feelings and issues arise. If one or both members of the partnership aren't being fulfilled or aren't reaching the heights of sexual gratification, then someone is holding out, someone is not in the game."

Jeff shared with me the following about a client that he had and his experience with his wife. For the purposes of this example, we'll call the man Martin and the woman Susan. Jeff said that Martin was quite Blue and Yellow, similar to me. Jeff then said that Susan was Teal and Yellow, which is fairly close to my wife's identity profile. The similarities peaked my interest. Jeff said the client told him about a conversation that went on between Martin and Susan:

Jeff said, "First, I have to set this up for you. Martin asked for sex and even tried to seduce Susan the previous day. But she's very Teal and likes to have a lot going on. 'You're not going to get it today,' Susan told Martin.

Martin was not feeling that great about where they were in their relationship. In fact, Martin would often run various victim patterns in his mind about how he wasn't good enough, and what if he ignored all of her needs, and why is it that she never acted excited to be with him until they were in the heat of the moment?

Martin got up the next day and helped around the house. This guy was persistent as many of us are when we want it. He asked again and she replied, 'Maybe I'll be able to squeeze you in my schedule.' Martin's wife also said that the day was one of those 'clean the house days,' so Martin pitched in for several hours to make sure the house looked nice. In most ways, Martin is an optimist, and I'm sure he was thinking that his help would score some points with Susan. He also stayed home with the kids while she went grocery shopping. To Susan's credit, when she came home from shopping, she realized how much Martin had been helping her. She said, 'Thanks honey for your help today, I really appreciate it.'

It's interesting to look at their different motivations here too. Martin was doing all of these 'extra' things for Susan, because he wanted to show her that he loved her. Meanwhile, Susan just thinks they should be done, because they need to be done.

She was happy they were done, but in her own mind, it wasn't a matter of love to her.

Well the day turned to night and my client, Martin, was getting a little anxious, because he knew his wife had also been running 90 miles an hour and that she'd be tired. And being tired meant no romantic encounter. Susan let Martin know that she remembered her statement to him and said, "Maybe we can do it, if the kids are in bed early."

Susan remembered that she had a presentation to give the next day and she felt she needed to work on it. The younger kids were in bed, but it was Friday night and the teenage son would need to be picked up from a friend's home.

Jeff smiled at me and said, "Well you're starting to get the picture, aren't you? Martin gets home a little after 10 p.m. He's a little dirty and sticky from the day's activities and he decides to take a bath to relax his sore muscles. He still holds out a little hope, but not much, on the idea of a romantic interlude." Jeff holds his finger to his temple, "Remember that I told you that Susan is a Teal. Well, she likes structure and order and likes to have things planned out. Martin's realizing how this plays out in their relationship. Martin knows his wife's schedule and how he'll have to wait another couple days for a good opportunity. Martin was frustrated about life and all the hassles, but he was carrying that over to his wife, because she kept on putting things in front of him. Being a Blue, Martin wears his emotions on his sleeve – well, more on his arm now, because he's in the tub. So now you know the set up to the conversation that is about to take place. Susan walks into the bathroom and finds Martin soaking in the tub.

'Are you mad at me?' She asks with a little venom in her voice. She had planned on giving him what he wanted, but now he was in the tub and she was tired, she thought he was sulking. And in a way, Martin was sulking and playing the victim role.

'Well, now that you mention it, I guess I'm kind of irritated! It's gone until this point and now I'm sure you're tired and want to go to bed.'

'Yeah, well I offered! I'm sure that whatever it is, it's all my fault!' Susan goes to bed upset, while Martin continues to wonder what on earth he's supposed to do. It seems to him that he just can't win. And when he expresses himself, she feels guilty and then says, 'I guess it must be my fault!'

Martin decides to get out of the tub, gets his PJs on and goes to his home office. Susan shows up in his office door about ten minutes later. 'I'm sorry, I've been feeling depressed. I don't know what it is with me? I hate the way I am in our relationship! I'm the only one that can get me out of it! I'm feeling terrible and you won't talk to me.'

This was becoming quite a raw conversation and some very deep emotions were surfacing for Martin and his wife. This is where Martin could have run some old patterns and he would have ended up in either a worse place or would have made up with Susan and received the immediate love he wanted or he could choose to step back and implement a deeper, co-creative communication that would help him improve his overall relationship. He responded by going deep. 'I don't know how to talk to you. How I'm experiencing this is that every time I bring up how I feel, you start to feel like you're the problem. You start feeling like the victim.'

Susan went back to the same place and said, 'But I am the victim, because I'm the problem.'

He could sense her pain and said, 'But it's really our problem.' Martin and Susan decided to go back up to the bedroom to continue their discussion.

Martin and Susan laid on their bed and pushed through some of the tears and the unmet feelings of love and talked through what they were feeling. Martin remarked, 'There is no way you can love me the way I need, unless you love yourself first.' When Jeff related this, it struck a nerve, because my wife and I had had this very same conversation about if we don't love ourselves, we can't love each other.

Susan asked, 'Tell me five things I can do to show you that I love you?'

Martin said, 'I don't know about five things, but I just want to feel loved when it comes to sex. Why is it that you won't ever ask for it like you want it? Instead it's always an offer or a task to mark off your checklist. You even said that when you stormed out of the bathroom – 'I offered it to you!' Can't we just make love, because we both want to love and be loved?' Jeff then pointed out how right-brained this

200

guy was and how he just wanted to be loved for who he is.

'I wouldn't offer it, if I didn't want it,' she said, still on the defensive.

'But the way I experience it is that you don't ask for it like you want it.'

'I guess I'm not the lover you want.'

Jeff said that Martin was now getting a very in depth look at his wife and her feelings and why she resisted him. Martin said, 'You used to want it and you used to want me. And you came after me to get it!'

Susan replied, 'Yeah, what was that, nearly thirteen years ago before we had kids? It's just not me anymore.'

Jeff said, "Martin told me afterwards that at this point in the conversation he was thinking, 'Why was it you then?' And he was questioning whether she had lost her love for him."

Jeff continued, "Here's where Martin presented his thoughts and feelings and why he was always feeling neglected. He said, 'I don't want you to give me sex. I want you to want sex and I want you to want me... and then give me love. I don't want to be another item on your checklist. I don't want to feel like another burden to you.'"

His wife replied, "Sex is just the tip of the iceberg. There are more problems than that."

Jeff said, "I could tell that Martin was growing because he told me he didn't jump to any conclusions with Susan's last comment. He simply acknowledged it and said, 'Yeah, I guess sex is one of those deep-seated needs, isn't it? And when it surfaces, it comes up with all sorts of emotions.' Martin told me that there was a long pause before either of them spoke. Finally, Martin said to Susan, 'I love you and I will do what it takes so that you feel my love for you.' Martin and Susan talked for a little while longer and then decided to kiss and hold each other and then go to sleep."

Jeff said that his comment to Martin was that he needed to count this as a big win in having a breakthrough in communication with his wife. He also said that Martin often would get upset and hold back from communicating and when he would communicate, he'd either get angry or he'd get too choked up and emotional to express himself. Jeff said, "That is very common among very Blue people." I related to this experience strongly, because I often do the same with my wife. I could empathize with the reaction of withdrawing or having emotional outbursts.

Within a few days after my session with Jeff, I had a very similar experience with my wife. It was almost like déjà vu. I remember lying in bed after the discussion, feeling like I'd had a similar breakthrough with my communications with my wife. I also remember talking about some of the other emotional issues, like the progress at my karate studio. I said, "I feel like I'm living between my dream and reality."

My wife said, "I know and it scares me and I've been having panic attacks over it! I've also been having bad dreams! I just don't know what to think."

I distinctly remember being at the verge of tears and then pleading for help from above, "Help me…Strengthen my unbelief!" And then I felt more calm and said to my wife, "I don't have the answers, but I have some faith." I had the thought to kneel down with my wife in prayer together, like we used to do more often when we were first married. After our heartfelt prayer, we kissed, embraced and then went to sleep.

So how does this play into the concept of leadership? Until you're ready to put yourself in the game with someone else, you really can't lead. And until you're willing to take responsibility for your own feelings and actions, you can't expect anyone to jump in the game with you. Both in the case of Martin and Susan and my wife and me, we were willing to be in the game no matter the cost and to find out how we could help the other person win so we could win. That is teamwork, which is a winning relationship – being fully and completely in the game because of your passion to win and to help the other person win. You have to be in the game to win and to help others win to really be a leader who leads with love motivation.

I Can't Win Without You Behind Me

In the Cliff Hollingsworth screenplay and Ron Howard film, *Cinderella Man*, the real life characters of James J. Braddock and his wife, Jane are in the middle of the Great Depression and are struggling to keep their family together, food on the table, and the heat and lights on. James Braddock breaks his hand and loses his license to box. But after healing, he gets a miraculous opportunity to fight the number two heavyweight contender, in which he shocks everyone by knocking John "Corn" Griffen out in the third round.

Braddock's manager, Joe Gould gets him another fight versus John Henry Lewis. Before James leaves for the fight, he goes to kiss his wife and says, "I know this isn't what you wanted, but I can't win without you behind me."

"I'm always behind you," she says.

James wins two more fights and becomes the top contender to become the Heavyweight Champion of the world. His opponent is the reigning world champion, Max Baer, a man who has the reputation of having killed two men in the ring.

When Jane Braddock realizes that James may die in the ring, there is a very emotional conversation. She begs James not to take the fight, even if he has to break his hand again. She says that she used to pray so that he'd get hurt, just enough so he couldn't fight anymore, because she was afraid of him dying in the ring. She tells James that when they took his license away, she was scared about their dire situation, but she went to the church and thanked God.

How is that for having conflicting intentions? He wants to win to provide a better life for his family and his wife wants him to get injured, so he can't fight or win?

The conversation reaches a climax, where James tries to dismiss her fears and she heatedly says, "He's killed two men Jimmy! What's worth it, huh? What's worth it?"

James responds, "I have to believe I have some kind of say over our lives... okay. You know... that things are bad, that we can change 'em... that we can make things better for our family."

Jane tells him how she needs him and that she needs him to be safe. And his reply is that nothing is safe anymore. I can almost hear my wife and me having the same discussion about what I'm doing with my career. She wants safety and I don't see safety in working in the corporate world. Yet, I need her to be behind me or I feel like I can't win either.

I get the feeling that plenty was said without words and felt without release during the time leading up to the championship fight. Even when they said goodbye, before he left for the fight, Jane and James' eyes locked and plenty was said without a sound between them.

Jane runs their three kids over to her sister's and goes to the church to pray for Jimmy. As Jane enters the church, she sees how many people her husband has touched by beating the odds. The priest tells her, "They all think that Jim's fighting for them." And so did the whole nation in the time of the Great Depression when heroes who represented millions of beaten and downtrodden people were hard to find.

Jane goes to see James and finding him in his locker room she says, "Maybe I understand some about having to fight. So you just remember who you are, you're the Bulldog of Bergen, and the Pride of New Jersey, you're everybody's hope and you're your kids' hero. And you are the champion of my heart, James J. Braddock." I honestly believe that had she not communicated her intention and her vision of who he was in her life and the life of her kids, he wouldn't have had a shot at the title. That is how much power two people can co-create together.

Although James J. Braddock, both in the movie and in real life, is a hero, it's Jane's lines that say it all. These are the words she says – you are a hero to your kids, you make a difference in the world, and you are the champion of my heart – that's what every man or woman needs burned into his or her heart and soul before they go out every day to conquer the world – to slay their dragons. Every man or woman who goes off to face their fight, needs that kind of support and to feel worthy of their cause, of their purpose. That is the message that Jeff was giving me about every man needs to teach their spouse how to love them, so that they too, can go out and fight the Max Baers of the world or slay their dragons. If your spouse isn't successful, then based on results, you're not successful. And that fact, that truth, shows up everywhere.

Jeff would sometimes refer to scriptural references based on my religious beliefs. When we were talking about relationships to our wives he said, "I believe in the principle of the target. If you want to get as close to a person's teachings, who is no longer with us, find the person that was closest to him or her in life. In the case of Jesus Christ, that would be Peter. So if we go to Peter to find out how we should treat our spouses, we can find a pretty good answer in 1 Peter 3. But I don't want you to go to the King James version (the translation I'm used to reading), because it shows a little less love toward the female spouse." Jeff had me go online and go to a more modern translation of the Bible (NIV). In 1 Peter 3 it says:

> 3 Your beauty should not come from outward adornment, such as braided hair and the wearing of gold jewelry and fine clothes.
> 4 Instead, it should be that of your inner self, the unfading beauty of a gentle and quiet spirit, which is of great worth in God's sight.
> 5 For this is the way the holy women of the past who put their hope in God used to make themselves beautiful. They were submissive to their own husbands,
> 6 like Sarah, who obeyed Abraham and called him her master. You are her daughters if you do what is right and do not give way to fear.
> 7 Husbands, in the same way be considerate as you live with your wives, and treat them with respect as the weaker partner and as heirs with you of the gracious gift of life, so that nothing will hinder your prayers.

There is plenty of wisdom in these passages. First, that inner beauty is more important and doesn't fade. This passage also mentions that the wife is submissive through love, but that the husbands should treat their wife with respect, so that together you can gain the gracious gift of life (to co-create). The wives should also not give way to fear. With that said, the point Jeff wanted to make comes at the end of verse seven. "*...so that nothing will hinder your prayers.*"

"In other words," Jeff said, "That your desires and intentions can be manifested. If you don't co-create and support each other, the answers to your prayers or the daily miracles of life will be hindered or will cease altogether. That's a pretty big thing isn't it? That's why so many people get stuck in their business lives and in other aspects of life – because they're stuck with conflicting emotions and stories in their personal relationships with their spouses. The scripture gave me a new meaning to the phrase, "Behind every great man is an even greater woman." The man can't be great without the woman behind him, seeing him and treating him as if he is a superhero. And the woman won't have the energy to support the man as a superhero, if the man doesn't give the woman enough love and energy so she feels like treating him like a superhero.

It's just like the phrase Jeff told me, "You can't give away what you don't own, if you try to give it away you'll be stealing and soon you'll become emotionally bankrupt." So if your wife isn't giving you the love you need, then it's up to you to teach your wife how to love herself, so she can have an abundance of love to give back to you. And the very same thing goes if your husband doesn't have enough love for himself, ladies you need to help them love themselves, so they have an abundance of love to cherish and care for you the way you want them to. It honors the law of fair exchange in the Universe – you get what you give.

Sometimes you lead by following or supporting, but this role is still a leadership role and those who master it silently lead others in life. You are a leader by seeing greater possibilities in others and affirming their potential. Somehow the magic of co-creation takes over and you experience what you desire most – because others are seeing you succeed in their minds.

Goal Systems That Help You See And Emotionalize Success

Part of leading is having the vision that creates passion, both in yourself and in others. In order to create the vision and communicate it, you need a good way to define your goals. However, the way you set your goals should be tailored to your personality rather than some advice from another person. For many left-brained people it's more important to have checklists and a linear way to accomplish goals. For many right-brained people, it's important to have visual connections to goals, such as a mind-map or a board of pictures that represent the accomplishment of the goals.

I've been through plenty of goal setting programs and I've had success with a few. I'm very right-brained, mostly blue. I'm not one to schedule every moment of every day. I developed a better understanding about my preferred patterns from reading my personality profile. The best goal setting I've done in the past is setting a goal for the year and then working on it every day. Believe it or not, I'm one that makes New Year's resolutions and then keeps only one of them. I've made resolutions to read from inspirational books every day. Another year I made a resolution to write in a journal every day. And yet another year, I made a resolution with my two oldest children to not eat candy for a full year. In each case, it took a commitment every day to make it happen.

There is nothing wondrous about any of these yearlong goals; I don't really consider myself a great goal setter and an overachiever. I just work on one thing on a daily basis. Sooner or later I achieve my goal. In that same vein, my best results for achieving everyday goals is to use a planner or smartphone and set down some "Roles and Goals" as Stephen Covey calls them. Then I know what I need to accomplish and hopefully I can work on the important things during each week. I often feel like I don't really commit whole-heartedly to a goal. Yet, I know that I can achieve great things when I put my mind to it.

So what is it that makes me commit? It's being able to see the whole goal and emotionalize the success and let the details fill in as I go. I'd say what makes me commit is a passion that I can truly visualize in my mind. I have to see it first, then experience the excitement of achieving it in my mind, and then I'll do it. Jeff would later tell me that this is how right-brained people achieve most things in life. They have to see it and experience it before they can take action. On the other hand, left-brained people have an idea and then take action on the idea and then experience the emotions of success as it unfolds and as the results come in. I also need the freedom to choose my goals for myself. I don't like to adopt goals from others. There's something inside of me that won't let me commit to someone else's goals until those goals become mine and even then, I like to tweak things for me, so I can call them my own.

Like so many new ideas for me, there is a point of enlightenment and then there is a long string of connections that go off in my head. Knowing what I wanted – to open a karate studio and to be a freelance writer – and going through that first leadership training with Jeff set me on a crash course to making my dreams a reality. But having a dream and putting it down in such a way that it becomes a reality takes more than writing it down in a planner or smartphone for me. I wanted goals that helped me visualize the results I wanted. It was at the end of the my initial training with Jeff when our product management team used whatever method fit our personalities to put our goals down so we could each see the goals clearly. I chose a mind mapping method.

I took each of my goals I had pared down from a pool of many desires and drew a little picture in the center of a paper. Then I wrote down the most important steps to reaching that goal. From there I branched out to include anything I could think of that came off those key areas. Soon I had a tremendous amount of my goal visually in front of me. I did this mind-mapping goal-setting exercise for each of my key life areas – Career, Family, Physical, Social, Mental and Spiritual… Once I had the goals visualized, it was easier to write down the things I needed to get done in my digital to-do list.

Each area that branched off the simple drawing of a karate person kicking in the air had to do with a different area of making my dream come true. There was one branch that was about the business organization, another about me as a teacher and karate practitioner, another one for the location and build out, and one for marketing and promotion. I found it enlightening that I could so quickly draw out every step I needed to take in order to successfully open and run my karate studio. This method also made it easy for me to see if there were any missing steps. With enough room on the paper, I could even start putting dates down and get a general feel for possible critical paths or bottleneck areas.

With all of my goals and tasks outlined and written in To Do lists, I created a business plan and a financial prospectus to project my income and growth. Now with my documented vision in place, I started to take action and people started showing up for me. I'm constantly amazed at how easily everything came together. Looking back, it seems that the stronger my intention and vision was, the more the Universe helped me manifest my vision.

Making It Crystal Clear

1) There are three layers or levels to leadership:
   - You must lead yourself before you lead others.
   - You must be a great follower.
   - You need to know when to lead others and do so with passion.

2) Greater awareness of your major weakness or kryptonite will lead to greater moments of learning and growth in your relationships. How do you experience your major weakness in your relationships?

3) Use a goal system that fits your personality – left-brained people need more linear process like checklists and 'To-Do' lists while right-brained people need more visual experiences like mind maps and visual boards with pictures of their goals, i.e. pictures of a desired automobile, home or happy family.

Intentional Vision Exercises

1) Share at least three wins with someone close to you, who

you haven't shared wins with before.

2) Create a list of people who will be willing to help you win at your game of life.

3) Create an affirmation to remind yourself of the truth about what you fear – that you are really the opposite of what you fear.

Chapter 8

Embracing Your Kryptonite – Owning Your Life

Don't Stop Seeing Angels and Superheroes

> *"We are like angels with just one wing.*
> *We can only fly by embracing each other."*
> – Anonymous

The previous quote is fascinating when you think that we are often a right-winged or rather a right-brained person, looking for a left-winged or a left-brained person. If we connect and lift each other, there is no limit to what we can do or accomplish.

In the spring, I asked my wife if she would allow me to take her through the Intentional Vision life-coaching process. To my surprise, she said "Yes." In retrospect, I believe I wanted the experience more than she did, but then that's how I saw it. I was excited and honored to be able to take my wife through such an enlightening experience.

I gave her the reading assignments and the exercises. For the first few weeks she made it through the homework, but expressed that the homework seemed more business oriented and therefore hard to follow at times. She felt she had to translate to relate it to her life. She was right, the earlier versions were adapted more from business training materials. I continued to encourage her and to tell her, "I'll love you through it."

There were some emotional moments that we had together as we went through the experience. I remember helping her see things a little differently. For example, we have a family in our area and the father, Michael, runs an Opera Festival every summer. It is reportedly one of the top places in the world to experience an opera or a musical. Laurie, Michael's wife, called my wife and said that my youngest son came up for a part in the musical, *Annie Get Your Gun*.

My youngest son was eight and had never done anything theatrical, so why his name came up is beyond either my wife's or my understanding. Nevertheless, here was an offer for him to experience something completely different. My youngest son hasn't been very focused and he often wanders around in his imagination. I've had him in karate, and although it has been helpful, he hadn't experienced the same self-discipline and focus others have.

My wife could just see in her mind that he would be all over the place and that he'd probably screw up when on stage and it would embarrass her. I could see she was experiencing the pain and fear in her own mind and she was doubting his ability to perform with professionals.

We talked about seeing our son doing really well and seeing him taking his bow after having the performance of his life. I think she started to see it just a little. I also reassured her that there was a reason his name came up for Michael's family.

My wife decided to go along with the opportunity. She took our son in for an audition and an interview with Michael. He was intrigued and inquisitive and interacted with the adults, asking lots of questions and showing a maturity beyond his years. Michael said that there was no question that he was the one for the part.

My wife worked closely with our son to memorize his lines and he had them down by the time rehearsals started. It was very quickly apparent that our son had a reason and a purpose to be there. He took to the theater like a natural and many of the professional actors and singers complimented him on his poise and ability to perform.

The time came for his first performance. My wife and I shared duties as stage parents, waiting in the wings. After our son gave his first lines in his first scene, he came off the stage and said, "That was easy!" I don't think he missed a line in all eight performances and he developed a great relationship with the lead actors, Joy Hermalyn and Mark Walters.

My wife saw our son doing well in her mind and it quickly put her worries to rest. The more she saw him succeed the more she manifested it as a win for her. She no longer saw him as a child who couldn't focus and do something. This was but one experience she manifested during our coaching sessions.

I felt a greater closeness and love with my wife, something that I hadn't felt since the year when we opened the karate studio together. I felt her support and we would find a purpose together, beyond the usual life in marriage and parenthood.

It was in our fourth session, during that time when the imprinted mind unleashes all sorts of challenges, I had a strong feeling that she needed to go through an exercise where she writes her name on a paper and then the names of four or five other people on separate pages. She then placed the papers on the floor anywhere in the room in relation to the paper with her name. She placed the papers close to hers. I said, "Now stand on your paper and look at one of the other names." She looked at our youngest daughter's name. "Now ask that person, 'Why are you here?'"

My wife interpreted that as, "Why are you here on earth or why are you here in my life?" I honestly meant, "Why are you here… to talk to me?" Tears welled up in my wife's eyes. She turned her head away to hide the emotions. Then she ran into the bathroom. When she returned, she had covered up her emotions and was like a stone statue. There wasn't any emotion expressed as she talked to the other people on the pages. It was a short experience and as Jeff would say, "It was a perfect experience." Yet, something happened to me as much as it happened to my wife.

Right after that experience, my wife said that she was going to be too busy in the summer to continue doing the life coaching. She was focused on making my younger son successful. He had a very intense rehearsal and performance schedule. I specifically remember, almost as if she was dropped down from a higher place, I stopped looking at her as an angel all because of what I was expecting out of the experience. I obviously still had much to learn about "loving her through it."

It was a very frustrating summer for me. I felt let down. I felt guilty for the problem. I somehow held her accountable for giving up and not continuing. I also remember it not being a very intimate summer. Yes, it was busy, but in my mind, you make time for what's important. I didn't feel important in her eyes, and maybe in mine as well. This whole experience was just me reacting to my major weakness. I felt I was being judged and rejected. I remember we had more than a few rough conversations and feelings. Looking back, it was still a perfect learning experience for me although at the time I felt like I was losing ground in my personal progression.

Again, my business, after making a decent leap in the number of students, began to plateau. I thought I could pull myself out of the slump at the end of the summer and in the fall. After all, that had been the best time for people signing up in past years. I spent plenty of money on advertising in the movie theaters, on the radio, with an anniversary event, and on mailers. Nothing worked and I can make up plenty of reasons in my mind, but I didn't grow during that time.

I felt a greater level of awareness and I was still learning and making plenty of "epiphanistic" connections with my world, but I was also experiencing fear within my relationship and therefore in my business world. In other words, my mind was growing in awareness and knowledge, but I felt that my heart was shrinking and stagnating. Like any other time, the experience drew my wife and I back to another heart-to-heart conversation. Our discussion was so deep and it convinced me that it was there for a reason, something I needed to learn from. I wrote the following in my journal:

Serious Conversations
November 14

"I didn't wake up this morning feeling this way." Her frustration and emotions were leaking out from under her wall. "I feel terrible! Here you let me go off for a weekend and I appreciated it, but I don't want to come back! I just need to accept that this is the way things are going to be in our family. I have to accept that I didn't marry someone who is going to earn a lot of money!"

My wife doesn't feel secure about our financial situation and our future. I'm not exactly on top of the financial heap and I'm struggling to keep a positive, abundant attitude about it. "I know I haven't provided the security you want. I'm working on it but…" I didn't really know how to end that statement, so I let it hang out there…

…I remembered that emotion that came up, of how I tend to think about focusing on one thing and then having to make a sacrifice in another part of my life. I said to my wife, "I'm working on seeing myself succeeding in all areas of my life. I just know that if we can improve our relationship, I'm going to have greater success at the studio."

My wife responded, "You see, that's what I don't like! I don't like carrying the burden of your success or failure. It's your dream, not mine."

I remembered Jeff saying to me that I needed to make sure I expressed my feeling through the phrase of, "This is my experience…" Keeping that in mind, I decided I'd step out on the limb and tell her how I have experienced the last year. I told her again, "Please don't feel guilty for any of this, it was just how I experienced it."

I groaned within. There were too many chicken-and-egg relationships going on. How do I communicate to her that I'm not judging her in that way? I just need to feel like she's behind me and I've already seen how I've won when I felt she was supporting me. When I say that I need her support in order to succeed in business, she would take that as I'm blaming her if I don't win. She would talk about how bad things were and I'd try to help her see that there was hope and a positive future. She didn't want to hear the hope, she wanted me to fix the problem, now! I felt like if I could just succeed a little more, then maybe she'd see the success and give me more support. I was looking for a win-win or co-creative situation and the problem is that we were both looking at it in different ways.

I said, "Do you want to know how I have experienced the last year with the karate studio?" My wife kept doing small things around the kitchen as we talked. I hoped that she would stop, but I decided to let it go. "I remember feeling that we were making progress when I first started taking you through a life-coaching process. And then we got to that neural-linguistic exercise where you stood on your paper with other papers representing different people's names on them. I asked you to ask our youngest daughter, 'Why are you here?' You melted. Your emotions rushed to the surface and you ran into the bathroom. Somewhere along the way, you made a decision that you didn't want to feel these new emotions, so you tucked them away. When you came back to finish the exercise, you were like a stone statue. And that was the end of our life-coaching sessions.

I blamed you for that experience. I blamed you for shutting down and shutting me out. That was in the spring and I felt shut out even more during the summer. There was very little intimacy between us and it ate at me. It wasn't until after we had a heart-felt discussion at the end of the summer, that I realized I'd been judging you. Where I had previously set you up as an angel, on a pedestal, now I had taken you down. You were no longer an angel in my mind. Again, don't blame yourself, it was our experience and it was how I was looking at you that made the difference. I wasn't holding you up as the angel I know you are. I was judging you. I was blaming you. Now I'm not. You are an angel. You are my angel!" The last part I spoke softly and through tears. I choked up with emotion as I heard my own words come out.

    I really did feel my wife's pain. I felt I could even understand her point of view. I had been experiencing a great deal of stress too and I couldn't put my hand on it. My jaw was tight and had ached for days. I didn't have the same energy or desire to exercise. I thought it was strange though, I had been having all sorts of new inspiration, awareness and connections in the last couple of weeks, but there was a void in my heart and spirit. I just wasn't sure how I could win when it seemed that we were neutralizing each other. I was working to see abundance and it appeared that she was always dealing with scarcity. You just can't win when you're neutralizing each other.

    I expressed to my wife, "I wish I could set our relationship aside and just go for it and make it happen (like a Red personality would), but I can't operate like that, unless it's from the heart. And then it hit me. Maybe there was a better way to look at this. Maybe I just needed to see or experience how my wife was supporting me."

    "What can I do?" she asked." If you can't

articulate what I'm supposed to do to show my support, then how am I going to fix it?" I was stumped. It was an emotion I was looking for from my wife, it wasn't an action. Yet, that's where we often get stuck. She wants something to do and I want to experience an emotion.

I paused to reflect and it came to my mind what I needed to ask her to do. "I need you to envision me succeeding on a regular basis and I need to be able to relive my wins with you." That's what I felt was missing. When she was helping me with the studio during our first 18 months, I felt her help and support and I felt that she was experiencing success with me. It wasn't something from her mind or even something that could be accomplished with her busy hands, it was something from the heart.

"You can talk with me about the business." She said, "I think you need to manage your business more and you just need to be doing more marketing or some more advertising, and I don't mind talking to you about that."

"I spent more on advertising this summer and fall than I ever have and I ended up with less. I did an event that should have gone over great, but it didn't give me the results I wanted. Can't you see that if my heart isn't in it, whatever it is, it won't work? I can't manifest it."

I continued, "I think I just need to see you in a different way and experience your support in a different way. It's really the What-You-See-Is-What-You-Get principle at work here. It's my faith and intention. I can honestly say that if it's not both in my heart and in my mind, there just won't be any magic.

I look back over my life and there aren't that many examples of when I committed everything I had to something, not in school, not in my career, and not even within my church responsibilities. I probably committed more to sports and physical activities than anything. But, I committed my whole soul to making the karate studio happen and there was nothing but miracles that happened in that experience. And that happened again when I went through this Intentional Vision life-coaching process the second time. It just happened. There is no reason why in that short period of time I gained 25 to 30 new students!"

I moved up to the counter so I could look my wife in the eyes. "If there is any blame, it is with me. I have let my old fears of scarcity creep back into my life. It's my Kryptonite of not committing because of the fear of being judged and rejected that is keeping me from achieving my goals – it's not you. But you sure can help me see and feel it differently."

We exchanged some personal words while in each other's arms that confirmed we understood each other.

As I look back over our conversation, it happened for a reason. I also feel a degree of peace and relaxation. Although my wife said she didn't wake up that day feeling depressed about her life, it was brewing underneath in the subconscious or imprinted mind. There was pain and emotion, but I felt that we had a win because we left the conversation with a connection and a better understanding. I also felt it was a personal win because throughout the conversation I felt like I kept my wife in a place of higher love. I respected what she was experiencing and I never judged her as anything less than the angel I know she is.

If you can own your emotions and the experiences, no matter who they are with, you will find an amazing harmony in your closest relationships. See it from a different angle; see the person as an angel or a superhero. I mentioned how I said to my wife that, "I'll just love you through it." Well that is exactly what we all have to do in this life experience.

Finding the Lost Ring

Right around the time of the previous discussion with my wife, my daughter was digging around in the recesses of a couch and saw something shiny. It was my wedding ring. Finding the ring coincided with my new awareness that I had dropped my wife down off her angelic place. Because of that awareness I was now placing her back up in a higher position in my mind and heart. My wedding ring had been lost for two years, but this would start us on a road back to trust and love for each other.

My wife immediately came down to the studio and placed it on my key ring. I was surprised to see the gold ring among my keys and I thought maybe my wife was giving me a new ring. I was amazed to hold the ring up and notice its slight S-curve. It was my old ring! To me this was a manifestation that things were going to change for my wife and me. I let many of my feelings of anger toward my wife fall away, but there was still more that I had to let go.

Since that previous discussion, I've placed my wife back up on an even higher pedestal and I look at her as an angel. It's extremely unusual that I take my wife down from that higher place of love in my heart and mind. That doesn't mean we don't have our disagreements, but it does mean that I view them differently and I don't hold her in contempt for anything she says to me.

By the way, shortly after this, I experienced greater success at the studio. We had a better December than all the previous Decembers we'd had. My outlook for the New Year was great. We were improving both the number of students and the level of my leadership team.

Like so much of my life, I wouldn't trade the experiences of these last few years of self-discovery and awareness for anything, even with all the fear and anxiety that came with it. I've grown more and received more awareness in my life during this time than any other time in my life. I am grateful for my wife, for her support, for her love and help in my life.

During the previous spring, when I had held my wife up in my mind and heart as an angel, I wrote the following:

> Why Did You Marry Mommy?
> March 19
>
> My youngest daughter asked me the same question that she asked me a little while ago. I think I even wrote about it one day in February; however, since I've lost my February journal entries [computer crash], I guess I'll never know. She asked, "Daddy, why did you marry mom?"
> "Because I love her, I think she's cute, she is a good mommy, she makes me laugh, she likes to go to movies and to plays with me, she likes to travel, and I think she's the greatest." I thought that was a fairly good list of reasons. My daughter thought so too, because she didn't follow up with any other questions. She just slipped between the sheets and acted like she might fall asleep.
> I was glad my daughter asked that question. It's nice to think about all the wonderful reasons why you love someone. My wife thinks that it's hard to love her. That's not really true. I think it's pretty easy, to tell you the truth.

You have to continue seeing people as something they can and will be. You have to see them as angels and superheroes. I've created an affirmation to help me keep people in a higher state of mind and heart. I now say, "I live in a beautiful world with angels and superheroes. I love to witness their superhuman potential and their miraculous powers and I enjoy sharing with them just how awesome they are!"

Superman Owned His Wheelchair

> *"I believe we each live in a world we've created in our own minds, and of which we are the center; and of course, the happy people are the ones who are satisfied with the world they own."*
> – Clyde Braegger – Polio survivor who lived his whole life in a wheelchair.

> *"He never walked, it's true; He spread his wings – and flew."*
> – Pat Braegger – Polio survivor who spent her entire adult life living happily in a wheelchair alongside her husband Clyde

What's amazing about going through the Intentional Vision process is that everything seems linked together. For instance, I would watch TV and there were all sorts of things that would jump out at me about the power of intention or whether someone was motivated by fear or motivated by money and power. Everything in my life seemed to fit together. The pieces snapped together right in front of my eyes. I was in this state of mind one night when I was up late watching TV. I often do that when I'm not committed to tomorrow. It's a bad habit that lets me escape from life a little. I go in spurts when I do it until I realize that it doesn't serve my purpose. However, this one particular night it did serve my purpose.

Oprah Winfrey came on. Now most guys won't admit that they enjoy watching Oprah Winfrey. Well I'm quite Blue, so I'm not one of them. I think she's awesome and I appreciate her passion and purpose to make a difference in people's lives. That's why this particular show caught my attention. She was interviewing Dana Reeve, the wife of Christopher Reeve, the big screen Superman and a real life Superman.

I've always admired Christopher Reeve and his battle with his overwhelming disability. I was heart struck when I first heard he'd suffered the spinal injury several years ago. I remember thinking,

"What would I do if I was completely paralyzed?" The answer I thought about was, "I'd rather die than go through that experience." Christopher Reeve, the Superman actor, faced his Kryptonite.

As much as I've admired Christopher for his courage, I have also been lifted by Christopher's wife, Dana, and her dedication and love for her husband. I was touched and brought to tears with some of the reflections Dana had about her husband. But there was one quote Dana said about Christopher that, to me, defined how he found ownership in his life. Enough that he could go on to make a difference in other people's lives.

Dana said that right after his horse riding accident that paralyzed him from the neck down, Christopher said, "I could trade my life with a bum on the street and be happy, because I thought, 'I can't live like this…' I would give everything up just to be able to walk again, to move again." Then Dana said that near the end of his life, Christopher said, "And now, I wouldn't trade my life with anyone. I have my family. I have this life. I've made a difference."

A great thought from Christopher Reeve is this one: "There are always people who are worse off than you are. The best thing to do is simply not complain, but just get on with your situation, whatever it is, and go forward, period."

Tears ran down my face as I heard the voice of Christopher through his wife, Dana. I couldn't comprehend the type of love she had for her husband. I wiped the tears away and continued to marvel as to why I'd chosen to stay up late this night. I thought to myself, "Christopher Reeve made a difference because that was his purpose. Would he have made as great a difference if he hadn't been paralyzed, who's to say? However, I believe that he chose this life experience before he came here as well as he chose Dana to be a part of his extraordinary experience. He lived out a beautiful, meaningful life that touched everyone around him. I want to do that. I really want to do that!"

I believe this life experience is a spiritual experience that gives us the ability to identify with a greater eternal perspective, giving us hope and intention toward the eternities. I knew Dana felt that same way, when later in Oprah's interview, they showed a clip from Dana's farewell remarks to Christopher at his funeral. Dana said, "I made a vow to Chris when we married that I would love him and I would be with him in sickness and in health, and I did okay with that. But there's another vow that I need to amend today. I promised to love, honor and cherish him till death do us part. Well, I can't do that, because I will love, honor and cherish him forever. Goodbye to you." And she blew him a kiss.

If Dana saw and believed she would be with Christopher forever, I believe that a loving God will permit her to do so. If love can only be measured by self-agency or the ability to choose, then love after this life experience is still based on choice. This is why I believe that love and choice are the fabric of the eternal realm – What-You-See-Is-What-You-Get is how we co-create with our Creator. Dana saw love without bounds with Christopher and that love, along with her husband, await her beyond this life experience. In the eternal sense, they were only separated by mere moments.

Dana developed lung cancer and died only months after Christopher. I'm happy she fulfilled her promise to Christopher to love, honor and cherish him even beyond this existence. I'm not sure anyone can look at her death and not see their love and not believe that they were soul mates with a purpose to change the lives of everyone around them. This world would be a much poorer place without a Superman and an Angel like Christopher and Dana Reeve.

How is it that someone in a wheelchair can live with great love in their hearts to the point that no one could be in their presence without being touched? We all have wheelchairs or weaknesses but it's not whether or not anyone can see them, it's how do we see them in our lives. Do we own our wheelchairs? When we do, life is wonderful. When you don't own your wheelchair, it owns you and will consume you.

Do we have to pass through such trials as the Reeves to experience such deep love and appreciation for each other and for the people that surround us? The answer is absolutely not. You can be happy with who you are right now. You can be happy with your position in life if you find your purpose in life, increase your intentional vision to achieve your purpose, and open your heart to yourself and others. It's only a matter of what you see life to be.

Tale of Two Eagles

Remember the story earlier in the book about the eagle that thought he was a chicken? Well the story didn't end when he took off from the farmer's arm. He soared into the sky and was almost overwhelmed by the beauty that lay above and below. He danced along the updrafts on the western sides of the mountains. He found peace in his soul and beauty everywhere he looked. He only stopped soaring to land and rest for the night.

The next morning the eagle took flight once again and soared higher than before, reaching heights where it was hard to breath and that made him dizzy. He opened his mouth to proclaim his joy and an eagle's screech came out. His insides tingled and he couldn't imagine life any other way. He landed toward dusk on a dead tree branch near the top of a high mountain.

On the following day he took to the sky, swooping down into a mountain valley and up over another peak. He still had the same joy of soaring, but something inside him was missing. There was also another hunger, he hadn't eaten in two days and he wasn't quite sure what he should eat, now that he was a true eagle.

He soared down a mountain slope and saw another eagle, a female eagle perched on a high tree branch. He landed on a branch on the other side of the tree. He saw that the female eagle was looking very intently down on the valley floor. "What are you looking at?" he asked.

"Shhhh," the female eagle said. "I'm watching for that rabbit to come out of its hole."

"Why, what are you going to do?" the eagle asked.

The female eagle took its eyes off the rabbit hole and looked at him in disbelief. "What do you think? I'm going to invite the rabbit out for dinner, my dinner!"

The eagle thought to himself, "I've got to see this, maybe this is what I need to do to eat."

The female eagle looked back at the rabbit hole. The brown rabbit had come out and scampered a few feet from its hole. The female eagle spread her wings and like a thin line along the horizon dropped down into the valley. At the last moment, when it was too late for the rabbit, the eagle tilted its wings back and landed directly on the unsuspecting hare. When the kill was made, the eagle flew back up the mountain to the same tree.

"Wow, that was awesome! I've got to try that!" Again the female eagle gave him a funny look and began eating. The eagle scanned the valley. He saw a large wood chuck scurry out of its burrow. "Do we eat those things too?" he asked. The female eagle looked out across the valley and nodded its head. The eagle took off and started his descent just like the female eagle had. He loved the speed, but began to wonder if he was going to crash and end up in a heap of feathers. His thoughts made him unsteady and before he could get close enough, the woodchuck darted back into its hole.

The eagle pulled up abruptly, abandoning his attack. He flew straight back to the tree where the other eagle was still feeding. "That's harder than it looked," the eagle said to the female eagle. "How do you stay so steady?"

"I just don't think about it," the female eagle replied.

"Hey, I'm pretty hungry. I haven't eaten for days and I've never eaten anything like that. Would you mind if…"

"Get your own, bud. I worked hard for this!"

"I'm not sure who I am or what I should do?" The eagle said to the female eagle, a hint of despair in his voice.

The female eagle paused from eating, looked at the eagle, searching to see if he was telling the truth. The female eagle could see the confusion in his eyes and decided to help him. "What is it you want?" the female eagle asked.

"I just learned to fly a few days ago. I'm not sure I can do what you just did." the eagle said.

The female eagle sat there dumbfounded, "You just learned to fly? Well you're doing pretty well for just learning to fly."

"All I know is that I've spent my life living with chickens and now I can fly."

The female eagle was still trying to take in this stranger who had shown up. The female eagle said, "You need to come with me." The female eagle sprang from the branch with wings outstretched. The eagle took to the air, following close behind the female eagle. The two flew down to a lake in the valley and glided along the surface. The female eagle called out, "Look at yourself in the lake." The surface was like a mirror and the eagle could see himself for the first time. The sight of himself up so close made him realize he wasn't a chicken with big wings, he truly was an eagle, born to fly, born to feel the freedom of the wind. He could see his bright yellow eyes gliding along in the lake. As he glided along, the female eagle broke the mirror surface with her talons and hooked a fish, snatching it from its watery home.

The eagle was amazed at how talented this female eagle was and how effortlessly she caught food. They flew to the top of a large tree overlooking the lake. The female eagle ate the fish as the eagle looked on, hunger pangs shooting through him as he watched. But he kept his peace and waited to learn more from his new friend. When the female eagle had finished eating, the eagle broke in, "I don't think I can ever be as good as you."

The female eagle smiled and said, "You're just like me, you're just a guy and I'm a girl. There's no other difference." He looked surprised and realized there had been a different feeling around this female eagle. Now he was even more interested to learn from her and about her.

The next few days, as the eagle's hunger pangs grew, he wondered if he'd made the right decision in leaving the chicken coop. "At least back on the farm I wasn't starving," he thought. "I wonder if the farmer would take me back?"

The eagle spotted a small rabbit in the foothills on the ground. Without thinking, his hunger driving him, he swept down on the unsuspecting animal and instincts took over. It tasted great, both the victory and the nourishment. He was so hungry that he ate the rabbit on the ground. Without knowing it, a coyote had slipped up behind him when he was only half way done with his meal. The eagle turned his head to see a vicious animal charging at him. He took off, but without his prized meal.

The eagle flew back up to the tree, where the female eagle was. She chortled, "Nice attack, bad choice of dining locations."

"I was so hungry, I didn't care where I was eating."

"Yeah, but you do now, don't you? Listen, I'm willing to help you out a little, you know, teach you a few things, but you have to give me some of what you catch."

"That sounds great. When can we start?"

"Right now! You're lucky, there's something over there by that large juniper tree." The eagle looked and saw a large ground squirrel. He almost took off immediately, but the female said, "Make sure you come out of the sun, it will be hard for it to see you."

"Thanks." The eagle took off and like his last hunt, he was successful. He flew back to the tree with the ground squirrel. "How much of this thing do you want?"

"This one's on me," she replied.

The two eagles hunted together for a few weeks and he became very adept at seeing and seizing the opportunity. Although his belly was full, his heart wasn't. He took to soaring more and more. Meanwhile, the female stayed to her perches and watched for more prey.

The eagle would come back from his flights, with bigger and bigger prey. "You really need to come with me and see some of the world, it's beautiful up above the higher mountains."

"No, what's the point of all that soaring. I'd rather keep my eyes open for prey."

"Well, you can also do that but from higher up, riding the clouds. It's beautiful and when you're hungry, things just come out wherever you are."

"Don't you know that eagles don't do that around here? We just work the same area over and over and we always get enough to survive."

"That's ridiculous! Why wouldn't you want to enjoy the beauty that's all around you?"

"It's not what we do?"

"Well it's what I do," said the eagle. He left the large rabbit on the branch near her and said, "You can have that one. I've already had plenty."

The next morning the eagle took to the skies. The female waited patiently for something to appear. Nothing came out. She began to worry a little. The eagle came back that evening with another large meal. Again, she wondered where he was getting all the food. He didn't eat and said that he'd already eaten his fill. He just thought she might want something, since food in the valley wasn't as plentiful as it used to be.

The eagle tried again to get the female to soar with him. "Can't you see I'm busy?" she said. "Why don't you go get some other eagle to soar with you?"

He looked puzzled at her and then thought, "Why not?" He took off and let the winds carry him away. He spotted a couple more eagles in a nearby mountain valley. They were perched and on the lookout. He swooped up and landed gently next to one of the eagles. "You know," he said, "why don't you guys come fly with me? It's fun to soar up over all the mountain ridges and dance on the wind and in the sun."

"Can't you see that we're busy trying to catch food to live on?" said the largest eagle.

"You mean you don't like to soar either?"

"Why would we want to soar, when all the food is closer to us here? We just have to swoop down and grab it."

"She was right, all the eagles just want to catch food," he thought. "This is crazy! I've got to go back and convince her to come with me."

The eagle flew back to the valley. The female was hungry, but he didn't bring her anything this time. "If your soaring method is so great, why didn't you bring me back something?" she chided him. She was upset because she started to believe that by helping this eagle catch food, there wasn't enough food for her now. He held his peace.

The next morning, the female spotted a large rabbit. She looked around and the eagle was gone, so she took to the air. She worried that maybe she might miss this one and she wavered a little in her flight. Still, the rabbit didn't notice its impending doom. Just before she was about to strike, the eagle swooped across and scared the rabbit back to its hole at the base of a tree.

She was livid. "What did you do that for? That was the biggest rabbit I've seen in weeks," she called after him.

He flew higher and called back to her, "Come with me!" The sky was blue and vibrant. She chased after him, as much to take a nip at his tail feathers, as to see what he was going to show her. He flew higher and higher. She caught up to him and he said, "Look down!" She looked down and it took her breath away. The mountains seemed to go forever.

"I never knew it was this beautiful up here. I thought if you got up this high, you wouldn't be able to come back down. I'd heard that there were strong winds up here that would carry you away. At least that's what my parents told me."

"There are strong winds up here, but that's what makes it so easy to soar. Come with me," he screeched at her. She followed, this time at his wing tips. They swooped down into the valley where the other eagles were sitting. They sped past them so closely that one nearly fell off his branch. The two eagles laughed at the looks on their faces. Then the eagle led his female friend up to a peak. The wind swelled beneath them and they began to rise higher and higher.

"I'm afraid!" she cried out.

"You'll be okay. You're with me and I've been here before." She followed as her heart raced. They soared for hours around the highest peaks. She'd completely forgotten her hunger. But he remembered and led her back down. They spotted several animals and could easily take their pick.

The eagle that once thought he was a chicken and his companion who had been afraid to soar, became great teachers to their offspring and the other eagles in that region. Now anytime you go to the wild mountainous regions, you may be lucky to see a majestic eagle soar, a descendant of the eagle that thought he was a chicken.

You and I are like eagles who have been spending too long in the chicken coops of life. Don't get cooped up, spread your wings and fly. And with you, others will spread their wings too. Remember that the fear is there to teach you about love.

When You Embrace Your Kryptonite, You Become The Master

The point of the story about the eagle who thought he was a chicken is how we all are when we come into this life experience. We don't know our potential and what's worse is that we only see the world through our set of glasses with our major weakness obscuring our vision. Yet, it is when we embrace our major weakness that we are led to experience the best in our relationships and life. We begin to see with clarity and truth.

Once you've embraced your major weakness and allow it to show you how to experience love and abundance, you become the master and you will be able to teach others how to look at life differently.

You'll help expose belief patterns that no longer serve your friends and neighbors in their lives.

Life mastery is simply about mastering the fear that stands between you and the love, abundance and passion you want to experience in life. Master your kryptonite and you master your life.

Final Affirmation

As you reach the end of this book and start your own journey or just find a better way to continue on your current path, I offer you a final affirmation in the form of a poem; a poem called "The Psalm of Life" by Henry Wadsworth Longfellow:

> Tell me not, in mournful numbers,
>   Life is but an empty dream! –
> For the soul is dead that slumbers,
>   And things are not what they seem.
>
> Life is real! Life is earnest!
>   And the grave is not its goal:
> Dust thou art, to dust returnest,
>   Was not spoken of the soul.
>
> Not enjoyment, and not sorrow,
>   Is our destined end or way;
> But to act, that each tomorrow
>   Find us farther than today.
>
> Art is long, and Time is fleeting,
>   And our hearts, though stout and brave,
> Still, like muffled drums, are beating
>   Funeral marches to the grave.
>
> In the world's broad field of battle,
>   In the bivouac of Life,
> Be not like dumb, driven cattle!
>   Be a hero in the strife!

> Trust no Future, howe'er pleasant!
> Let the dead Past bury its dead!
> Act, – act in the living Present!
> Heart within, and God o'erhead!
>
> Lives of great men all remind us
> We can make our lives sublime,
> And, departing, leave behind us
> Footprints on the sands of time;
>
> Footprints, that perhaps another,
> Sailing o'er life's solemn main,
> A forlorn and shipwrecked brother,
> Seeing, shall take heart again.
>
> Let us, then be up and doing,
> With a heart for any fate;
> Still achieving, still pursuing,
> Learn to labor and to wait.

This is one of my father's favorite poems. This poem influenced many in past generations, including Henry Ford and even Mohandas Gandhi. Gandhi quoted a favorite passage from this poem, "...*things are not what they seem*," only days before he died.

Longfellow penned these lines while in the depths of despair. He had bought the house where George Washington had once lived and he found himself one day standing at a window of a room that used to be Washington's office. Longfellow's wife had died three years earlier and he was living in what seemed like an empty dream.

It was while standing at that window, wondering what Washington must have gone through, that Longfellow willed himself to do something to break out of his depression and by doing so, he penned one of the most beloved poems of the late nineteenth and early twentieth centuries. He broke out of his depression because he started to see things through the eyes of former heroes, such as George Washington.

Like Henry Wadsworth Longfellow and others before him, may you live like an Angel or Superhero by experiencing the love that comes from owning your life.

May we also "leave behind us footprints on the sands of time" so others may follow. At the end of every coaching series, Jeff and I challenge our students who are graduating to put it out to the Universe that they get to share this Intentional Vision journey with someone else. This challenge holds true with this book as well. As you finish reading, invite others into your experience and go through it again. You'll find that your enlightenment, understanding and connection with love and the divine will grow as you do this with a close neighbor, friend or family member.

May God bless you with love and abundance as you live a more intentional life. Carpe Diem Amore! Seize the day with love and make it your superhero day!

Making It Crystal Clear

1) Embrace your kryptonite and be a superhero or angel.
2) Master your major weakness and you master your life.
3) Teach what you have learned about your major weakness and allow others to grow in their awareness.
4) Invite others to join you in this experience.
5) Act as a superhero and you become one.

Intentional Vision Exercises

1) Teach a neighbor what you've learned – then let go and let God accomplish miracles in your life and theirs.

Epilogue

Jeff and I hope you found this book to be both enlightening and life affirming. You are truly someone with potential and power. To live with love and purpose is to live without fear. Learning to trust God, the Universe or another power greater than you in life is the start to a life filled with love, energy, creativity and success.

Trusting that you have a purpose in life and trusting yourself in this life experience is the next step to success. Finally, when you have learned and accepted the power of trust between you and your source of creation, you can easily trust that others are there to help you and you are there to help them in serving a mutual purpose. When you trust life and others at a higher level, and you repeat the process, you become an unstoppable force in the universe. You will attract at an even faster rate the people and circumstances to serve your purpose. You will be able to co-create the life you're intending.

This book only represents a few of the lessons I learned while going through this Intentional Vision life strategies program with Jeff. There are layers upon layers of learning that I've experienced relating to the lessons Jeff taught me. It would be nearly impossible to describe all of the learning and love I've gained over the last seven years. However, I know that I at least need to share with the world another part of the experience I had with Jeff.

The Kryptonite Factor sets the foundational principles for growth. The next book, The Co-Creation Equation, gives you an even deeper look into how you can set your life up for success, no matter what experiences you're going through. In The Co-Creation Equation, we will go into more depth about the principles established in this book and we will include more exercises, so you can work through many of your thinking patterns and set yourself up for greater success. Additionally, we will discuss how to be a better leader, how the Universe can direct more energy your way when you put yourself out there, ways to set up your rules for success according to your personality, how to find and declare your soul purpose in life, how to use the Be-Do-Have with Purpose method for setting and achieving goals, and much more.

For more information about this upcoming *The Co-Creation Equation* book, please visit us at kryptonitefactor.com or coachingclarity.com.

www.ingramcontent.com/pod-product-compliance
Lightning Source LLC
Chambersburg PA
CBHW061637040426
42446CB00010B/1463